AUSTRALIAN HISTORY COMPREHENSION YEAR 6

Gunter Schymkiw

Five Senses Education Pty Ltd
2/195 Prospect Highway
Seven Hills 2147
New South Wales
Australia

Schymkiw, Gunter
Australian History Comprehension Year 6

ISBN 978-1-76032-163-5

CONTENTS

1. SIR JOSEPH BANKS

The highly regarded English seaman, Captain James Cook, sailed on a voyage of discovery and scientific investigation in his ship Endeavour. The voyage lasted from 1768 to 1770. It was Australia's good fortune that the young wealthy scientist by the name of Joseph Banks sailed with him. Banks saw that the continent, whose east coast they had explored and mapped, had infinite possibilities.

Joseph was born in London on 17th February, 1743. His father, William Banks was a wealthy landowner and member of the English parliament. From a very young age Joseph was keenly interested in learning. His special interest was science.

He spent many of his young hours studying the plants and animals that lived on his father's estate in Lincolnshire. Botany, the study of plants, held a particular fascination for him. Joseph began his schooling at the age of nine
at the highly regarded Harrow School. At thirteen he continued his schooling at the equally famous Eton School. Finally at the age of seventeen he finalised his formal learning at Oxford University. It was during his period at Oxford that his father died and Joseph inherited a large fortune.

James Cook

Managing this did not blunt his enthusiasm for the study of botany. At the young age of twenty-three he was invited to become a member of Britain's foremost scientific group, the Royal Society. The Society's chief aim was to improve knowledge of the natural world.

In the same year (1766) he made his first botanical exploration outside of England embarking on a voyage to the icy Canadian provinces of Labrador and Newfoundland. Learning a great deal, he was eager to undertake a similar excursion.

The Royal Society decided to provide funds for Captain Cook's expedition to observe the transit of Venus (when the planet Venus passes directly between the Sun and Earth)in the Pacific in 1768. Banks saw this as a tremendous opportunity to further natural studies. He offered to provide finances so that the natural history of the areas visited could also be studied. His offer was accepted and Banks joined this memorable voyage whose highlight was charting Australia's east coast. Banks found and catalogued many new plant and animal species in the places he visited, especially in the continent Cook named New South Wales.

Encouraged by this success, Banks was eager to join Cook on a similar second expedition but was unable to raise the necessary funding. Not long after, however, he joined another expedition to Iceland and the Hebrides Islands. This expedition, while successful, was to be his last. He decided instead to spend his time supporting scientists by lobbying for research funding and with improving his collection of preserved plant specimens and adding to his extensive library.

Banks had a great deal of faith in the future of the colony of New South Wales. He energetically recommended it as a place for a likely colony. This enthusiastic support had much to do with the British government sending a settlement party of soldiers and convicts there in 1788 under the command of Captain Arthur Philip.

His active interest in the progress of the colony lasted for the rest of his life. Banks was greatly troubled by the painful condition called gout in his older years. Over the last 14 years of his life he had little use of his legs.

In spite of this he carried on working tirelessly. He is remembered in the names of the Sydney suburbs of Banksia, Banksmeadow and Bankstown and the plant called the banksia. A type of seaweed called Neptune's Necklace has the scientific name of Hormosira banksii. His picture also appeared on the first Australian $5 note.

Sir Joseph Banks

When he died in 1820 aged 77 the man known by many as the Father Of Australia was mourned in the colony which he had done so much to help establish.

Comprehension

A. Write short answers below.

1. With whom did Joseph Banks sail on a voyage of scientific investigation from 1768 to 1770? _____

2. In which ship did Banks and Cook sail? _____

3. What was Joseph Banks'date of birth? _____

4. What study interested Joseph from a very young age? _____

5. Where was his father's estate? _____

6. What is the study of plants called? _____

7. Which two famous schools did Joseph attend? _____

8. Which university did he attend? _____

9. Which scientific group was Joseph invited to attend at the age of twenty-three ?

_____

10. Which two Canadian provinces did Joseph visit on his first botanical investigation?

_____

11. What is meant by the transit of Venus? _____

12. What was charted on this memorable journey?_____

13. Why was Banks unable to join Cook on a second expedition? _____

14. Where did Banks go on his second overseas expedition (two places) ?

_____

15. Which place did Banks think had a great future? _____

16. What happened in 1788 as a result of Banks's enthusiastic support?

_____

17. Who was in charge of the 1788 settlement in Australia? _____

18. Which painful condition did Banks suffer from in his older years? _____

19. Which three Sydney suburbs are named after him? _____

20. By which name was Banks known? _____

B. Write numerals inside the brackets so the place names are in alphabetical order. Number 1 is done.

a. Banksmeadow (_____)

b. Newfoundland (_____)

c. Australia (___1___)

d. Banksia (_____)

e. Labrador (_____)

f. Bankstown (_____)

g. Hebrides Islands (_____)

h. Iceland (_____)

C. Find words with these meanings in the text. Some letters are given.

1. luck __ o __ t __ __ __

2. the study of how the world works __ __ __ e __ c __

3. to make available __ __ o __ __ d __

4. improve __ u __ t __ e __

5. trying to influence government officials so they will provide funds for projects __ __ __ __ y __ __ g

Activity

The words in the word bank all have something to do with botany.

Match them with their meanings. The highlighted letters spell out the answers to the riddles below. Use an online dictionary to check meanings.

SUBURB	EXOTIC	COSMOPOLITAN	FOREST	PREFIX	FOETID	LEAVES
AVOCADO	PALM	FLORA	BIOLOGY	GRASSLAND	CHLOROPHYLL	
VENUS	LACKING	EPIDERMIS	DECIDUOUS	BOTANY		

A.

1. The __ __ __ __ __ __ __ tree is a native of Mexico.

2. A __ __ __ __ __ __ __ __ __ tree loses its leaves in the colder months.

3. __ __ __ __ __ __ is another name for plants.

4. __ __ __ __ __ __ is the study of plants.

5. Botany is also a __ __ __ __ __ __ of Sydney.

6. Botany is also called plant __ __ __ __ __ __ __.

7. Another word for __ __ __ __ __ __ __ __ is Savannah.

8. __ __ __ __ __ __ __ __ __ __ __ is the green colouring in plants.

9. The leaf of a fern or __ __ __ __ is called a frond.

10. In botany a plant distributed worldwide is said to be

   __ __ __ __ __ __ __ __ __ __ __ __.

11. Something with an unpleasant smell is said to be __ __ __ __ __ __.

12. Foliage is another word for __ __ __ __ __ __.

PUZZLE 1 : If I have eight oranges in one hand and nine oranges in another, what do I have?

ANSWER: __ __ __ __   __ __ __   __ __ __ __ __

B.

13. An __ __ __ __ __ __ plant is one that has been introduced from another country.

14. Because it eats insects, the __ __ __ __ __ fly trap is said to be insectivorous.

15. The prefix 'e' in science means __ __ __ __ __ __ __. For example, dentate means with teeth and edentate means without teeth.

16. The __ __ __ __ __ __ hetero means dissimilar.

17. The prefix epi- means on top of or above. Your __ __ __ __ __ __ __ __ __ __ is your skin.

18. A community of trees with long trunks is called a __ __ __ __ __ __ __.

PUZZLE 2 : Which plants are on the face of every person?

ANSWER: __ __ __ __ __ __

In the days before cameras, botanists had to be very good at sketching. Sketch three plants from your local area.

INDICATORS AND OUTCOMES	a. answers literal questions
	b. is able to alphabetise
	c. uses context to find the meaning of words

Napoleon

You learn most about a person when they are in a position of power or authority. It would be nice to think that a person given authority over others would be offered such responsibility because they were fair, caring and wise. That was certainly not the case with Major James Mudie, a landowner and former soldier in the early days of the colony of New South Wales.

As an army officer in England he was such a disastrous leader that he was ordered to resign. Having no income he sought work with a bookseller. Once again he showed a lack of judgment. He persuaded the bookseller that they could both become wealthy by making and selling commemorative medallions. The medallions celebrated the great leaders and battles of England's wars against the French Emperor, Napoleon. The public were not impressed. The partnership lost £10 000 ($20 000), an enormous amount at the time. Mudie and his partner joined the list of bankrupts.

Now, once again, finding himself penniless, Mudie was saved by a family friend, Sir Charles Forbes. He organized free passage to New South Wales for Mudie. Furthermore, when he arrived he was to be given a land grant of 870 hectares at Patrick's Plains on the Hunter River. Mudie named this property Castle Forbes in honour of Sir Charles.

In the twenty years that followed Mudie gained a reputation as a merciless flogger of convicts. Forced convict labourers at Castle Forbes were fed barely enough to keep them alive. He reached the height of brutality on November 5th, 1833 when he smirked as five of the thirty lags (convicts) he had working for him were hanged not far from his homestead. His hatred of convicts was legend. He was given the position of magistrate in Maitland (NSW). When speaking of convicts he said:' Indulgence merely impairs their usefulness. Punishment is justified even when reformation has been achieved because it acts as a deterrent to lower classes in England.'

Cat-o'-Nine-Tails

Mudie fed the convicts unlucky enough to be chosen to do forced labour at Castle Forbes on offal. Occasionally he would kill an old bullock and laugh as he watched the convicts, many of them toothless, struggle to eat the tough leathery meat. The flour he gave them was usually a mixture of grass seeds and the sweepings from the floor of the mill.

Driven to desperation by their poor treatment, six convicts seized some guns from a hut on the property and fled into the bush. They were caught by troopers near the Hawkesbury River. Five were hanged and the other was sentenced to life imprisonment at the harsh penal settlement on Norfolk Island. Mudie insisted that the hangings be carried out on his property. All the convicts working there were made to witness the mass hangings. They were warned that they would suffer the same cruel fate if they tried to escape. The five went to their deaths cursing the man who had led them to this dreadful end.

News of the madness taking place at Castle Forbes was spread by the colony's official newspaper, The Sydney Gazette. Mudie traced the blame for this to William Watt, a former convict. He found out that Watt had, for a brief period, lived with a convict woman. (This was an offence at the time.) His attempt to have Watt imprisoned failed when the matter went to court.

Mudie was enraged. He was happy to return to England to give evidence to a transportation committee in 1836. While in England he wrote a book, The Felonry Of New South Wales in 1837. In this book he attacked his many enemies in the colony.

When he returned to Sydney he was chased down George Street by the horsewhip wielding John Kinchela. Kinchela was one of the people Mudie had ridiculed in his book. When the matter went to court Kinchela was ordered to pay a £50 ($100) fine. So popular were Kinchela's actions that a public fund raised the money to pay the fine. Mudie was devastated by this. It was as if, for the first time, he understood how deeply despised he was. He returned to England where he remained living in obscurity until his death in 1852.

Mudie left no worthwhile mark on the history of New South Wales. All that remains is his reputation as a hateful and detested bully.

Comprehension

A. Write short answers below.

1. Why was Major Mudie asked to resign from his job as an English army officer?

    _____

2. With whom did Mudie work after resigning from the army? _____

3. What did he persuade the bookseller to make and sell? _____

4. What did the medallions commemorate? _____

5. How much money did this cost Mudie and his partner? _____

6. Which family friend helped Mudie after he became bankrupt? _____

7. How much land was he granted? _____

8. Whereabouts was this land? _____

9. What did Mudie name this property? _____

10. What is a lag? _____

11. What act of brutality was Mudie responsible for on 5th November, 1833?

    _____

12. Where was Mudie given the job of magistrate? _____

13. Why, according to Mudie, was punishment of convicts always justified, even if they had reformed themselves? _____

14. What is meant by 'the lower classes'? Highlight the best answer. _____

    a. short people

    b. lazy people   **e.** convicts

    c. poor people   **f.** lags

    d. senior citizens   **15.** From what was the flour at Castle

Forbes made? _____

16. What were toothless convicts sometimes given to eat? _____

17. What happened to the six convicts who tried to escape from Castle Forbes?

_____

18. What was the name of the colony's newspaper? _____

19. Who was responsible for informing the Gazette of the goings on at Castle Forbes?

_____

20. Of which crime was William Watt accused? _____

21. What was the name of Mudie's book? _____

22. Who chased Mudie down George Street, Sydney wielding a horsewhip?

_____

23. How do you know that many people supported Kinchela's actions? _____

24. When and where did James Mudie die? _____

B. Find words with these meanings in the text. Some letters are given.

1. and **2.** words that mean disliked: d__ __ __ __ __ e __ and d __ __ __ __ __ e __

3. manual workers __ __ b __ __ __ __ r __

4. smiled in an arrogant, self-satisfied manner   __ __ __ __ k __ d

5. a judge in a court for minor crimes __ a __ __ __ __ r __ __ __

Activity

The words in the word bank all have something to do with crime or punishment.

Match them with their meanings. The highlighted letters spell out the name of the Russian author who wrote the famous book, *Crime And Punishment*. Write his name on the lines provided below. Use an online dictionary to check word meanings.

vandal	trespass	polygamy	jaywalking	community	libel
assault	hijacking	fine	arson	blasphemy	prevaricate
	offence	collar	fraud	bribery	

1. An amount of money paid for committing an offence is called a __ __ __ __.

2. __ __ __ __ __ __ __ __ __ is the crossing of a road in a dangerous manner at a place where cars do not usually stop.

3. Someone who criminally sets fire to property is committing the crime of __ __ __▬ __.

4. A __ __ __▬ __ __ is someone who deliberately damages another person's property.

5. The term white __▬ __ __ __ __ crime refers to crime carried out by a worker at a clerical workplace. These crimes typically involve a form of fraud.

6. __ __ __ __ __▬ __ is the crime of offering money or gifts to someone in return for them doing something dishonest or illegal.

7. To intentionally deceive someone for criminal personal gain is to commit __ __ __ __▬.

8. Rather than imprisoning criminals for minor crimes some authorities allow them to perform unpaid work that will benefit the public. We call the service they perform __ __▬ __ __ __ __ __ service.

9. __ __ __ __▬ __ __ __ __ __ is another word for swearing.

10. To __▬ __ __ __ __ __ __ __ is to enter someone's property illegally.

11. An __▬ __ __ __ __ __ __ is another word for a crime.

12. To publish false information about someone is to commit the crime of __ __ __ __▬ __.

13. To __ __ __▬ __ __ __ __ __ __ __ is to speak or act falsely or evasively with the intention of deceiving a person or people.

14. To __▬ __ __ __ __ __ someone is to make a physical attack on them.

15. __ __ __ __ __▬ __ __ __ is the act of illegally seizing a means of transport and using it for one's own purposes.

16. In Australia it is illegal to be married to more than one partner.
We call this __ __ __ __ __ __ __ __▬.

The author of *Crime And Punishment* is

▬▬ ▬▬ ▬▬ ▬▬ ▬▬ ▬▬   ▬▬ ▬▬ ▬▬ ▬▬ ▬▬ ▬▬ ▬▬ ▬▬ ▬▬ ▬▬.

Embezzlement is often associated with fraud. Write the dictionary meaning of embezzlement.

_____

INDICATORS AND OUTCOMES	a. answers literal and inferential (question 23) questions
	b. uses context to work out the meaning of words

3. PLAGUE IN SYDNEY !

There have been two great epidemics of the terrible disease, bubonic plague, in Europe. They took place in 1349 and 1666. In some places visited by the infestation more than half of the population died. There was an outbreak of this dreadful illness in Sydney in 1900.

The cause of the disease was unknown at that time. It was, however, known to occur in areas where rats were present in large numbers. Opinion was divided on how it spread to humans. Not all scientists agreed with the famous French researcher, Paul- Louis Simond, who believed that the illness was carried by fleas living on the bodies of infected rats.

Plague had been unknown in Australia up until that time. Medical authorities, however, had been informed as early as 1898 of outbreaks in the ports of Hong Kong, Japan, Malaysia, the Philippines and India. Trade vessels from these ports were involved in regular contact with Australian ports.

In December 1899 two ships from Noumea berthed in Sydney's Darling Harbour. Dead rats on board were collected and taken to the laboratories of Doctor John Thompson, the Government Medical Officer. When they were examined in the laboratories they were found to be riddled with plague.

An extermination campaign was immediately put into action but rat infestations were already firmly entrenched in some areas.

The plague claimed its first victim in January, 1900. Thirty–three year old Arthur Payne, a carter employed on the wharves at Darling Harbour, was rushed to hospital. He quickly succumbed to the terrible illness. In the eight weeks that followed there were few reports of cases of plague. The public, convinced that Payne's death was an isolated event, began to lose interest.

In late February, however, the disease claimed a sail maker whose workroom was located on the wharves. When the floorboards of his workshop were pulled up dozens of dead rats were found. The forty employees of the sail maker were gathered together and taken to the quarantine station on the North Head of Sydney Harbour. A short time later they were joined by fifteen tenants of a hotel in Sydney's King Street. The owner of the hotel had been drinking with his customers but had suddenly developed a fever, collapsed and died. The wharves and surrounding blocks were fumigated and people were told to stay away. Sanitary squads were employed to set traps and put down poison baits. By doing this 100 000 rats were exterminated. In spite of this the death toll continued to rise steadily.

Plague was a swift killer. The first symptoms were usually terrible headaches, fever and vomiting. This was usually followed by delirium (speaking in a deranged, incoherent manner). Finally the lymph nodes became swollen and pustulent black sores broke out on the skin. Often this all happened in a few hours.

The sanitary squads employed to halt the progress of the disease worked systematically, street by street, in the worst affected parts of Sydney. Householders were told to wash the woodwork of their houses with lime and carbolic acid. If they suspected any rat activity they were told to pull up their floorboards and lay poison baits. In spite of all this, new cases were being reported daily. People suspected of being in contact with plague victims continued to be sent to the quarantine station. More workers were employed to clean up slum districts.

It was feared that the pestilence could become widespread. Ships travelling from Sydney were believed to be the source of outbreaks in Brisbane, Rockhampton, Townsville, Melbourne and Fremantle.

Thanks to the efforts of the sanitary squads and the clearance of squalid slum areas the tide began to gradually turn. The last case of the illness in that outbreak was reported on 9th August of 1900. In all 303 people had been infected with the disease. Of these, 103 had died. There were other outbreaks of plague in 1902 and, most recently, in 1921.

Current day practices have made our cities less likely to be affected by plague. Nevertheless, nature is very inventive and our good health should never be taken for granted.

Comprehension

Write short answers below.

1. In which two years were there great plague epidemics in Europe? _____

2. In which year was the first Sydney outbreak of plague? _____

3. Who was the French scientist who thought that plague was spread by fleas living on infected rats? _____

4. In which five countries had there been outbreaks of plague in 1898?
   _____

5. From which country did the two rat infested ships of December 1899 come?
   _____

6. Who was the government medical officer at that time? _____

7. What did the bodies of the rats taken from these ships reveal? _____

8. What was immediately put into action? _____

9. Who was the first Sydney victim of the plague? _____

10. What was Arthur's job? _____

11. Who was the second Sydney plague victim? _____

12. Whereabouts in this man's workshop did they find the bodies of infected rats?
    _____

13. How many rats were killed as a result of rat trapping and poisoning campaigns?
    _____

14. Describe the symptoms in the first stage of plague. _____

15. Describe the symptoms in the second stage of plague. _____

16. Describe the symptoms in the final stage of plague. _____

17. How long does it take from onset of the disease to death? _____

18. What were people living in badly infested parts of Sydney advised to do to the woodwork of their houses? _____

19. Name five other Australian ports in which there were outbreaks of plague?

_____

20. When, in 1900, was the last case of plague in Sydney? _____

21. How many people were infected with plague in 1900? _____

22. How many people died during this outbreak? _____

23. In which two other years were there outbreaks of plague in Australia?

_____

24. Write a dictionary definition of PLAGUE._____

Activity

Match the health and sickness terms in the word bank with their meanings. Use an online dictionary to find meanings. The highlighted letters spell out the doctor's suggestion to his patient. One word is used twice in answer 3.

epidemic   ophthalmologist   sprain   zoonosis   vector   midwife   outbreak
malignant   infectious   fracture   antibiotic   surgeon   pandemic   chronic
incubation   mosquito   pathogen   thrombosis   mortality   diagnosis

1. A __ __ __ __ __ __ __ __ is any disease transmitted to humans by an animal with a backbone. Rabies is an example.

2. A disease that spreads from person to person is said to be __ __ __ __ __ __ __ __ __ __.

3. A __ __ __ __ __ __ is an animal that transmits a disease. The rat flea is a __ __ __ __ __ __ for bubonic plague.

4. An __ __ __ __ __ __ __ __ is an outbreak of a disease that spreads rapidly affecting many people.

5. A __ __ __ __ __ __ __ __ __ is an outbreak of a disease over a vast geographical area. A disease that spreads worldwide would have this label.

6. The __ __ __ __ __ __ __ __ is a vector for the disease , malaria.

7. The __ __ __ __ __ __ __ __ __ __ rate is the rate of death in a population.

8. A broken bone is referred to as a __ __ __ __ __ __ __ __.

9. An __ __ __ __ __ __ __ __ __ __ is a medicine that kills or limits the growth of harmful bacteria.

10. A __ __ __ __ __ __ __ __ is any small organism such as a virus or bacterium that can cause a disease.

11. The __ __ __ __ __ __ __ __ __ __ period of a sickness is the time between when someone becomes infected and when they begin showing signs of being ill.

12. The sudden violent beginning and spread of a disease is called an

    __ __ __ __ __ __ __ __.

13. An __ __ __ __ __ __ __ __ __ __ __ __ __ __ __ __ is a doctor who specialises in treating diseases of the eyes.

14. A __ __ __ __ __ __ __ __ is a doctor who performs operations by cutting the patient open.

15. A __ __ __ __ __ __ __ __ __ illness is one that is life threatening.

16. A __ __ __ __ __ __ __ __ illness is one that lasts for a very long time.

17. __ __ __ __ __ __ __ __ __ __ __ occurs when a blood clot stops blood flowing around the body.

18. A __ __ __ __ __ __ is an injury to a joint caused by a sudden wrenching or twisting of its ligaments. It is less serious than a break in bones but still very painful.

19. A __ __ __ __ __ __ __ __ __ is a doctor's judgement of the cause of a medical problem.

20. A __ __ __ __ __ __ __ is a person trained to help women in childbirth.

GIVE IT TO ME STRAIGHT, DOC

DOCTOR: I'm afraid you have a very serious illness. Do you have any questions?

PATIENT: Do you mind if I get a second opinion?

DOCTOR: __ __ __ __ ! __ __ __ __ __ __ __ __ __ __ __ __ __ __ __ __ __.

4. CHRISTMAS IN EARLY SYDNEY

Christmas, according to the well- known carol, is 'the season to be jolly.' To the earliest Europeans who colonized Australia these words would have had a hollow ring. Christmas in the colony in the first five years under Governor Phillip was anything but jolly. They were years of great hardship as the thousand or so convicts and soldiers struggled to eke out an existence.

Thoughts of Christmas in a friendlier environment — tables laden with all manner of foods, carolers singing in the streets, sitting cosily by a fireside, snow gently drifting down — these were all distant memories.

The stifling heat seemed to mock the misery felt by the new arrivals.

And what of the traditional Christmas feast? No matter how hard they tried to imagine it, none could convince themselves that the mouldy biscuits, salted meat and swigs of rum that they had were fit and proper Christmas fare.

The Christmas service in December 1788 was conducted by chaplain Richard Johnson. It took place under a gum tree near the colony's water supply, the Tank Stream.

On the next day, Boxing Day, the daily business of the penal colony resumed as always. One convict was sentenced to 200 lashes. A few days later another was hanged. Within a week another died of self-imposed starvation.

In spite of the general misery there were some brief glimpses of happiness in those first five Christmases. It was a favoured time for marriages. Recorded in the chronicles somewhere is the happy news that the governor's Christmas table included a rare treat — Lord Howe Island turtles.

Despite the risk of harsh punishment many of the convicts resorted to theft. Before he was hanged the convict, James Daley, named a woman whom he said had urged him to commit a crime. The authorities decided to make an example of her. On the following day her hair was shaved off and she was paraded before the assembled convicts in a canvas frock with the letters RSG painted on it. The convicts were warned that a similar fate was awaiting anyone else found guilty of being a Receiver of Stolen Goods.

Added to the disciplinary difficulties with the convicts were the constant visits of the curious aborigines. The clash of cultures between the European colonists and the indigenous inhabitants often resulted in hostilities.

Before the Christmas of 1789 the first crops at Rosehill (Parramatta) had been harvested. In spite of a 12 kilogram cabbage grown by Farmer Dodd there was nowhere near enough food to satisfy the hungry bellies of the colony's inhabitants. The chief topic of conversation around the Governor's table on Christmas Day, 1789 was the sad case of Lieutenant George Maxwell of the ship HMS Sirius. He had been declared 'completely insane' and was to be returned to England. No doubt, some of those left behind thought of him as 'Lucky Maxwell'.

The arrival of the second fleet in 1790 was after a nightmarish journey. Of the approximately one thousand sturdy souls who had set out from England more than two hundred and fifty had been dumped overboard in sea burials. Of the seven hundred and fifty or so survivors five hundred were admitted to the colony's overstretched hospital in George Street upon their arrival.

The Christmas of that year was somewhat better than that of the previous two years thanks to the arrival of a supply ship which brought with it thirty tonnes of rice, half a tonne of sugar and three hundred and fifty barrels of salted beef and pork. The Governor's table that year included the colony's first grapes. These had been grown from cuttings of South African vines. This was also the hottest Christmas experienced so far by the new colonists. The temperature reached 44°C. The hot winds blowing were described as being 'like the blast of a heated oven.'

On December 11, 1792, Governor Phillip began his return journey to England. He missed out on the bushfires that ravaged the colony that year. Leaving Australia's shores he must have carried with him many memories. It is doubtful that any of these would have included happy thoughts of Merry Christmases spent in the new colony.

Comprehension

A. Write short answers below.

1. What is a Christmas carol? _____

2. According to the Christmas carol, *Deck The Halls*, what is Christmas the season to be?

    _____

3. The people of the First Fleet came from England where Christmas is celebrated during winter. In which season is Christmas celebrated in Australia?

    _____

4. Food and drink play an important part in celebrating Christmas. List three things that made up Christmas fare for the newly arrived settlers to Australia.

    _____

5. Who conducted the Christmas church service of 1788? _____

6. Where was the service held? _____

7. What happened to one convict on Boxing Day, 1788? _____

8. What happened to another convict a few days after that? _____

9. What did another convict do about one week later? _____

10. What was Christmas the season for in the first five years of the settlement?

_____

11. What rare treat did Governor Phillip have on his Christmas table one year?

_____

12. What was the name of the convict who was urged by a woman to commit a crime?

_____

13. What happened to him? _____

14. How was the woman punished? List two things _____

15. What did RSG stand for? _____

16. How heavy was Farmer Dodd's prize cabbage? _____

17. What was Lieutenant Maxwell declared to be? _____

18. In which year did the Second Fleet arrive? _____

19. How many of the people who left England on the Second Fleet had sea burials?

_____

20. How many were admitted to the colony's small hospital when they arrived?

_____

21. From where did the colony's first grapes arrive? _____

22. List three other things that arrived with the Second Fleet. _____

23. To what temperature did the thermometer climb during the Christmas period of 1790? _____

24. What was it said the winds were like in that year? _____

25. When did Captain Phillip begin his journey back to England? _____

B. Think about modern day Christmas in Australia. List four foods that are commonly eaten by Australians celebrating Christmas. Highlight the one that you like the most.

_____

_____

Activity

A. Put the missing words from the Christmas Carol titles in their correct spaces. Choose words from the word bank. Four of the words are decoys. Use them on lines (B) to write a sentence about Christmas.

Gentlemen	Orient	Mary	Silent	Christmas	Manger	City
Joy	Sing	Drum	Tree	Donkey	Carols	Night

1. Away In A _____

2. _____ To The World

3. Little _____

4. God Rest Ye Merry _____

5. Carol Of The _____

6. O Christmas _____

7. Once In Royal David _____

8. The Seven Joys Of _____

9. _____ Night

10. We Three Kings Of _____ Are

B. _____

_____

C. Use the internet to answer these questions about the famous story, A Christmas *Carol*.

1. Who wrote this story? _____

2. In which great city do the events in the story take place? _____

3. What is the first name of Mr Scrooge? _____

4. Who is the crippled boy in the story? _____

D. Five of the books below were written by the author of *A Christmas Carol*. Highlight them. There are five decoys. Do not highlight them.

Black Beauty	Great Expectations	Oliver Twist	The Cat In The Hat
Bleak House	Fantastic Mister Fox	David Copperfield	Possum Magic
	Pickwick Papers	Animal Farm	

E. Design your own Christmas card below.

5. THE MYSTERY DISAPPEARANCE OF THE 'KICKING KANGAROO'

At the age of 15 young Pat O'Dea performed a feat that showed him to be a person of extraordinary courage and athleticism. Visiting Mordialloc Beach near Melbourne he saw a woman floating, seemingly unconscious, in the water. About thirty metres away a large shark was approaching her limp body. Without thinking of his own safety Pat entered the water and pulled the woman's body to shore. Sadly she had drowned after having a heart attack in the water. For his courage he was awarded a bronze medallion by the Royal Humane Society of Australasia. He was to receive many more awards in his lifetime.

Most of these were associated with his chosen sport — a game not well known in Australia. He came to be regarded as the greatest American Football (gridiron) player of all time.

Patrick John O'Dea was born on 16th March, 1872 in the Victorian town of Kilmore. The family moved to Melbourne and Patrick attended school at Xavier College. Being a naturally gifted athlete Patrick won selection in the school's senior Australian Rules eighteen. When he left school he played in the VFA (Victorian Football Association) for the Melbourne and Essendon clubs.

In 1895 Patrick enrolled in the study of law at England's famous Oxford University. On his way to England he decided to call in on his brother, Andy, who was studying at the University of Wisconsin in the USA. Patrick was very interested in his brother's accounts in letters of the unusual style of football played by the Americans. The field in this game is marked in a pattern like a gridiron used for grilling meat. The game, officially known as American Football, has come to be called gridiron by most people.

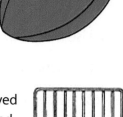

Gridiron for broiling

Arriving in Wisconsin he attended a few games as a spectator. Joining Andy watching the university team at training, Patrick picked up a ball and gave it a tremendous spiralling punt kick. On seeing this, the team's coach invited Patrick to join in the training session and was amazed at his kicking prowess and ball handling skill. Before long Patrick's plans had changed. He enrolled in a course at the University of Wisconsin and was picked to play in the university's gridiron team in the important position of quarterback.

Enthralling fans of the game with his prodigious kicking and clean passing, he came to be known as the Kicking Kangaroo. Kicking on the run, a fundamental move in Australian Rules Football, was unknown in the American game. Patrick's skill took Wisconsin to the top of the gridiron ladder. He decided that America would be his new home. After a distinguished career as a player his services were keenly sought as a coach.

He coached for several years at Notre Dame University in Indiana and then moved to the distinguished Stanford University in California. Despite his success as a coach Patrick became restless. He had wanted to establish a law practice in San Francisco but the demand for his coaching services interfered with this.

In 1917 the national hero disappeared mysteriously without a trace. There were many rumours concerning his disappearance. The most popular was that he had joined the Australian army as it had passed through San Francisco on the way to the World War I battle front in Europe. From time to time sightings were reported but for seventeen years Patrick O'Dea remained hidden from his adoring public.

In 1934 the sporting editor of the newspaper, The San Francisco Chronicle, Bill Leisler, was given an anonymous tip. He was told that if he wanted the sports story of the decade he should interview a man named Charles J Mitchell. Mitchell, Leisler was told, was an employee of a lumber company in the isolated Californian town of Westwood, about 240 kilometres North-West of San Francisco. Acting on this tip Leisler found that Mitchell was the long missing Patrick O'Dea. He convinced Pat to come out of his self-imposed exile.

'It just seemed a good idea to go away and leave the old life behind,' he told Leisler in an interview. 'Probably it was wrong to disappear but I wanted to get away from the mere student age of the past. As Pat O'Dea I seemed just an ex-Wisconsin football player. I decided to make a new life for myself under a new name.'

Patrick was uncertain of the reception he would receive but football fans welcomed him back with open arms at a homecoming celebration at the University of Wisconsin. He settled in San Francisco where he lived until his death following a brief illness in 1962. Among the many good wishes he received during his period in hospital was a get well message from the American President, John F Kennedy.

Comprehension

A. Write short answers below.

1. At which beach did Pat O'Dea pull a woman's body from the water? _____

2. Why was this act regarded as being particularly brave? _____

3. How old was Pat when he did this? _____

4. Which organisation presented him with a bronze medallion for courage?

_____

5. In which sport was Pat to excel (2 names) ? _____

6. When and where was Patrick born? _____

7. Which Melbourne school did Patrick attend? _____

8. For which two Victorian Football Association teams did Patrick play? _____

9. At which university did Pat enrol in 1895? _____

10. What did he intend to study? _____

11. At which US university was his brother enrolled? _____

12. Why is American football called gridiron? _____

13. What footballing skill of Patrick's impressed the coach of the Wisconsin University team? _____

14. Which important position did Patrick play for the University of Wisconsin team?

_____

15. What was Patrick's nickname? _____

16. What football related job did Patrick have when he retired as a player?

_____

17. Name two US teams that he coached. _____

18. What surprising thing happened to Patrick in 1917? _____

19. What did most people think he had done? _____

20. For how long was Patrick missing? _____

21. Of which newspaper was Bill Leisler the sporting editor? _____

22. Which name had Patrick used to hide his identity? _____

23. Where was he working? _____

24. How did football fans react when Patrick came out of hiding? _____

25. When did Patrick die? _____

26. Which US President sent him get well messages when he was in hospital ?

_____

B. In Australian football a goal (kick between the centre posts) is worth 6 points and a behind (kick between a side and centre post) is worth 1 point.

EXAMPLE: Collingwood scored 11 goals, 13 behinds. Their total score was (6 x 11) plus (13 x 1) 79.

Sydney scored 13 goals, 3 behinds. Their total score was _____

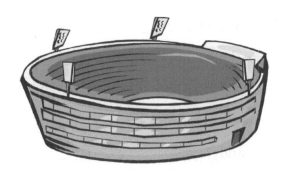

AUSTRALIAN SPORTING HEROES

Use the internet to find the answers below. Circle and highlight the answer you find to be correct. Don't guess.

1. The sportsman known as 'The Great White Shark'.
   (a) Kieren Perkins   **(b)** Greg Norman   **(c)** Rex Hunt   **(d)** Murray Rose

2. The Australian gridiron player who was known as 'The Kicking Kangaroo'.
   (a) Mal Meninga   **(b)** Harry Kewell   **(c)** Pat O'Dea   **(d)** Adam Goodes

3. Anne Sargeant was Australian team captain and excelled at this sport.
   (a) netball   **(b)** softball   **(c)** hockey   **(d)** badminton.

4. This cricketer is acknowledged as the world's greatest ever batsman.
   (a) Glen McGrath   **(b)** Don Bradman   **(c)** Steve Waugh **(d)** Bill Ponsford

5. This swimmer swam the English Channel nineteen times.
   (a) Suzy Maroney   **(b)** Dawn Fraser   **(c)** Ian Thorpe   **(d)** Des Renford

6. This Australian was the first woman in the world to win an Olympic gold medal.
   (a) Annette Kellerman   **(b)** Shane Gould   **(c)** Fanny Durack   **(d)** Tracey Wickham

7. In the 1980s and early 1990s there was a race run between Sydney and Melbourne called the 'Ultra Marathon'. Its first winner was in his sixties when he won. His name was…
   (a) Tony Rafferty   **(b)** Pat Farmer   **(c)** Cliff Young   **(d)** Ron Clarke

8. The only undefeated horse ever to win the Melbourne Cup was…
   (a) Black Caviar   **(b)** Grand Flaneur   **(c)** Phar Lap   **(d)** Makybe Diva

9. With 1 357 goals to his credit the highest all-time goal kicker in the Australian Football League is…
   (a) Gordon Coventry   **(b)** Jason Dunstall   **(c)** Jack 'Captain Blood' Dyer
   (d) Tony Lockett

10. This man's name is probably best known today for the tyre service company he began. He won medals for swimming at the 1908, 1920 and 1924 Olympics. He also rescued the victim of a shark attack at Sydney's Coogee Beach in 1922. He was…
    (a) Andrew 'Boy 'Charlton **(b)** Frank Beaurepaire **(c)** Jon Konrads **(d)** Grant Hackett

11. Pioneering Australian cricket commentator who inspired the song 'The Game Is Not The Same Without (Alan)…'
    (a) McGilvray   **(b)** Davidson   **(c)** Border   **(d)** Lawry

12. This man captained the yacht *Australia II* when it won the America's Cup in 1983. Prior to this US yachts had been unbeaten in 132 years of racing for the cup.
(**a**) Alan Bond   (**b**) Ben Lexcen   (**c**) Brucie Bailey (**d**) John Bertrand

13. This tall, thin, balding Rugby League champion played 18 seasons in England, scoring 796 tries.
(**a**) Brian Bevan   (**b**) Wally Lewis   (**c**) Dave Brown   (**d**) Brian 'Pop' Clay

14. This racing car driver and designer was world driving champion in 1959, 1960 and 1966.
(**a**) Alan Jones   (**b**) Vince Pirillo   (**c**) Sir Jack Brabham (**d**) Peter Brock

15. This jockey was the rider of the champion racehorse, Phar Lap.
(**a**) Jim Pike   (**b**) Darby Munro   (**c**) George Moore   (**d**) Damien Oliver

16. The world's greatest-ever billiards player who also raised over $6 million for charity in exhibition matches.
(**a**) Eddie Charlton   (**b**) Joe Davis   (**c**) Alex 'Hurricane' Higgins   (**d**) Walter Lindrum

17. This rower never lost a race in almost four decades of competition. In one race he stopped to let a duck and her ducklings cross in front of him, but still won easily.
(**a**) Edward Scanlon   (**b**) Henry 'Bobby' Pearce   (**c**) Grant Kenny
(**d**) Howard Croker

18. This squash player was beaten only twice in her career. She did not lose one match from 1962 to 1979.
(**a**) Lisa Martin   (**b**) Heather McKay   (**c**) Yvonne West (**d**) Nicol David

19. Australia's first female athletics 'star'. She was looked upon as a certainty to win three Olympic gold medals at the 1940 Tokyo Olympics. Unfortunately these games were cancelled because of World War II.
(**a**) Shirley Strickland   (**b**) Decima Norman   (**c**) Betty Cuthbert   (**d**) Raelene Boyle

20. This champion cyclist set many records. He is the only non-European to have won the Paris–Brest–Paris marathon. This race is so demanding that it is only held once every ten years.
(**a**) Russell Mockridge   (**b**) Martin Vinnicombe (**c**) Hubert Opperman
(**d**) Alfred Henry 'Professor' Tipper

21. Outstanding Rugby Union champions were Mark, Glen and Gary, known simply as the.....

(a) Waugh Twins   (b) Ella Brothers   (c) Chappell Brothers

(d) Earp Brothers

22. Champion Rugby League forward known simply as 'Big Artie' was Arthur.....

(a) Tunstall   (b) Summons   (c) Beetson   (d) Rank

23. Outstanding cyclist who won the incredibly gruelling Tour De France in 2011.

(a) Cadell Evans   (b) Major Taylor   (c) Stuart O'Grady   (d) Anna Meares

24. Australian Soccer player known as 'Roo'. He played for Liverpool in the English Premier League from 1981 to 1988, scoring a goal in the 1986 FA Cup.

(a) Johnny Warren   (b) Ray Baartz   (c) Harry Kewell   (d) Craig Johnston

25. World champion surfer in 1979, 1980, 1981 and 1982 was Newcastle's.....

(a) Mark Richards   (b) Bernard 'Midget' Farrelly   (c) Laine Beechley

(d) Nat Young

6. MATTHEW FLINDERS AND CAPTAIN PALMER – A HERO AND A COWARD

The early history of the European settlement of Australia is graced by the services of two of the great sailors and men of their time. Their names are well known to most Australians: Captain James Cook and Matthew Flinders. Cook, in 1770, was the first known European to find and map Australia's east coast. Flinders carried on from Cook and, in 1803, sailed around the continent and mapped much of its coastline. His journey proved that Australia was one large island. Many people had believed it consisted of two smaller islands. Like Cook, Flinders was not just an outstanding seaman. He was respected and admired by those who sailed under his command. Both men were regarded as being honourable and as caring deeply for the welfare of their men.

When Flinders returned to Sydney after circumnavigating (sailing around) Australia he planned to return to England and report on what he had learnt about the continent. The ship HMS Porpoise was made available to take him home. The vessel set sail on August 10th, heading northwards towards Torres Strait. Accompanying her were two merchantmen (ships which carried freight and passengers), HMS Cato and HMS Bridgewater. Little did they know on that first day what trials lay before them. A strong southerly wind drove the three vessels northwards at a frightening speed. By afternoon on the second day that wind had increased in strength to gale force. The sky became overcast and looked menacing as daylight gave way to darkness. Around 9.30 that night there was a sudden shout from the lookout of Porpoise 'Breakers ahead!' The crashing breakers were the belated warning of a reef that it was too late to avoid. The ship could not be turned from the reef that lay ahead. With a shuddering shock Porpoise struck it and was stuck fast and at the mercy of the waves. The Cato which was following close behind shared the same fate. The Bridgewater, following some distance behind, saw what had happened and had time to steer wide of the reef.

Matthew Flinders took over the command of Porpoise. A gig (long, light rowing boat) was thrown overboard and six sailors were picked to swim to it with Captain Flinders. Their aim was to paddle it to the Bridgewater to tell those on board what was happening and to inform its commander, Captain Palmer, of Flinders' plan for a rescue operation. As the gig neared the Bridgewater Flinders and the sailors were shocked to see it pulling away from them. In a short while its light had vanished into the night. No effort had been made by Captain Palmer to help Flinders and the stricken party of sailors and passengers.

They beached the gig on a spit (long, narrow strip of sand) close to the reef. Morning revealed it to be about one hundred metres long and fifty metres wide and bare of any vegetation. With no other option available to them Flinders and his men returned to the Porpoise which was still stuck fast on the reef. Using a roughly made raft they began transferring water and stores from the Porpoise and Cato to the sand spit. When the tide fell the passengers on the Cato were able to wade across and join them. The ordeal had cost three lives. Ninety-four people had  survived but their troubles were far from over. Flinders estimated that they were stranded about five hundred kilometres east of what is now the city of Rockhampton in Queensland.

The party had enough food and water to last for about three months. That would be more than enough to allow them to survive if Captain Palmer of the Bridgewater had alerted authorities and a rescue party had been sent. But could Palmer be trusted to do this? Why had he sailed away leaving them to more than likely perish without saying a word? No, he decided — such a man could not be relied upon! Flinders and his survival party set about repairing the remaining cutter of the two that was in the better condition. They had christened this boat the Hope. After working on the repairs for two weeks he, the captain of the Cato and twelve other seamen set sail back to Sydney, a journey of some 1 200 kilometres. As he had done so often in his life, Flinders rose to the responsibility that rested on his shoulders. Just thirteen days later the Hope passed through Sydney Heads. Arrangements were made to rescue the eighty who had remained behind on the reef. Their faith in the capability and honour of Captain Flinders had been rewarded and another chapter in an extraordinary life had been written.

Flinders was more than just a fine seaman. He was a good judge of men and character. With Palmer he made perhaps his best call. He was later to learn that when Palmer had reached the Indian city of Bombay (now Mumbai) he had written a report in which he had said that both the Porpoise and Cato had gone down with no survivors. As for the fate of Captain Palmer and the Bridgewater, after leaving Bombay's harbour the ship vanished without a trace and her captain and crew were never seen or heard of again.

Comprehension

A. Write short answers below.

1. What was James Cook first to do in 1770? _____

2. When did Flinders sail around and map much of Australia's coastline? _____

3. What did Flinders' journey prove? _____

4. What did people think Australia may have consisted of? _____

5. Why were Cook and Flinders admired and respected by the sailors who sailed with them? _____

6. On which ship did Flinders set sail to England? _____

7. Which two ships accompanied him?_____

8. What did Porpoise strike? _____

9. Which ship did not strike the reef? _____

10. What did Bridgewater do as Flinders' gig came near it?_____

11. Where was the gig beached?_____

12. How long and wide was the spit? _____

13. When did the passengers on Cato wade to the sand spit? _____

14. How many people lost their lives?_____

15. Approximately where were they stranded? _____

16. What did Flinders decide about Palmers' reliability? _____

17. What name had Flinders and his men given to the cutter that would sail back to Sydney? _____

18. How long did it take for the Hope to reach Sydney? _____

19. What had Palmer written concerning the fate of Cato and Porpoise? _____

20. What happened to Bridgewater when it left Mumbai harbour? _____

B. Matthew Flinders and Captain Palmer had differing values. Flinders was brave and selfless while Palmer appeared to think only of his own interests. The words in the word bank can be used to describe character. Write the good characteristics in the POSITIVE box. Write the bad characteristics in the NEGATIVE box.

traitorous	compassionate	helpful	apathetic	cowardly
		courageous		

POSITIVE:	
NEGATIVE:	

INDICATORS AND OUTCOMES	**a.** answers literal questions
	b. recognises how language can be used to create mood and imagery

Activity

The words in the word bank all have something to do with ships and boats.

Match them with their meanings. The highlighted letters spell out the answers to the riddles at the bottom of the activity. Use an online dictionary to check meanings.

bow	junk	log	aft	hawser	poop	berth	mariner	rudder
kayak	hull	blue peter	amidships	skipper	stern	wake		
sampan	starboard	bridge	rowlock	capstan	dreadnought			
brig	tramp steamer	conning tower						

1. A __ __ __ __ __ __ __ __ __ __ __ __ is a steamship that does not travel on any regular route. It is available for hire to travel and carry cargoes anywhere.

2. A __ __ __ __ __ __ is a strong, thick rope or cable used for towing or mooring (tying up) ships.

3. A __ __ __ __ __ __ is used to steer ships or boats. It is located at the back of these vessels.

4. If you are looking forward on a ship the __ __ __ __ __ __ __ __ __ side is on the right.

5. The __ __ __ __ is the frame or body of a ship. It is the part that floats in the water.

6. Another name for a sailor is a __ __ __ __ __ __ __.

7. A __ __ __ __ is the raised deck at the back of a ship or boat.

8. The __ __ __ is the very front part of a ship or boat.

9. The track of waves left by a ship as it moves through the water is the ship's __ __ __ __.

10. The back of a ship or boat is its __ __ __ __ __.

11. The back part of a ship is also known as __ __ __.

12. A __ __ __ __ __ __ is a small flat-bottomed boat, usually with a small cabin. It is powered by wooden oars.

13. A __ __ __ __ is a traditional large, flat bottomed Chinese boat with masts and sails.

14. The __ __ __ __ __ __ is an enclosed area above the main deck from which a ship is controlled.

15. The middle part of a ship is called __ __ __ __ __ __ __ __ __.

16. A __ __ __ __ __ is a small boat made of watertight skins stretched over a wooden frame and powered by a single paddle. These boats were traditionally used by the Inuit (or Eskimo) people.

17. A __ __ __ __ __ __ __ is a holder attached to the gunwale (the top edge of the side) of a boat. It holds the oar in place when the boat is being rowed.

18. The __ __ __ __ is the place prisoners are kept on US ships.

19. The __ __ __ __ __ __ __ __ __ __ __ __ of a submarine is the part from which the periscope sticks out.

20. A __ __ __ __ __ __ __ __ __ __ __ __ is a heavily armed battleship.

21. A __ __ __ __ is a day by day record of a ship's voyage.

22. A __ __ __ __ __ is a bed on a ship.

23. A __ __ __ __ __ __ __ __ __ __ is a flag with a blue border around a white square. It is flown to indicate that its ship is about to sail.

24. A slang word for the captain of a ship is __ __ __ __ __ __ __.

25. The anchor is winched up on a cable using a device called a __ __ __ __ __ __ __.

RIDDLES

A. The ship sank quite suddenly below the water and yet there was no panic. The people watching on the dock remained calm because __ . (Answers 1 to 20)

B. In the early days of European settlement in Australia the colony could not grow enough food to support itself. Supply ships carrying food were sent from England to make up the shortfall in foods. Most ships completed the harrowing voyage. The ship that consistently sank was the one carrying the colony's vegetables. Can you explain why? (Answers 21 to 25)
It was full of __ __ __ __ __.

7. THE AMAZING JOURNEY OF OSKAR SPECK

Oskar Speck was an enterprising young man. He had studied hard to become an electrical contractor. By 1932, aged just 25, he had built up a business that employed 21 people.

Unfortunately, however, Oskar lived in Germany which was still recovering from World War I. To make matters even worse, this was at the time of what was known as the Great Depression. All over the world businesses were closing and people were finding themselves without work. Oskar was forced to close his factory and join the millions of unemployed.

Although this was a great disappointment to him at the time, it was the cause of him undertaking a great adventure that would see him paddle, sail and carry a fold-up kayak that he had made, more than 50 000 kilometres. On this great journey, lasting more than seven years, he would see places he had never dreamed of seeing.

His initial aim was to paddle his kayak, the Sunnschien, down the Danube River and carry it overland to the Mediterranean Sea. His destination was Cyprus, where he hoped to get work in the copper mines. When he reached Cyprus, however, he decided that he was enjoying his lone adventure so much that he would continue it.

For the next seven years his paddle, a makeshift sail, feet and adventurous soul took him to many out of the way places. From Ulm in Germany he travelled down the Danube River then across the Middle East, to India and Sri Lanka, to Burma, Thailand, Malaysia, Indonesia, New Guinea and, finally, to Australia.

In Indonesia he was confronted by a group of local tribesmen who tied him up, kicked and beat him and stole most of his supplies. This beating left him with a burst ear drum.

When he reached New Guinea, in September 1939, he was surprised to learn that the world was, once more, at war.

Furthermore, because he had brought a camera to record some of the things he had seen, the Australian authorities there thought he was a spy. He was placed in an internment camp for the duration of the war (until 1945).

After the war Oskar decided to make Australia his new homeland. He went to live at Lightning Ridge in New South Wales, where he learnt the skill of opal cutting. His latter years were spent as a successful opal merchant in Sydney with his partner, Nancy Steel. He died in 1995. Items from his remarkable voyage are on display at the Australian National Maritime Museum in Darling Harbour, Sydney.

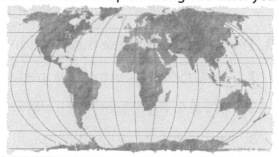

Comprehension

A. Write short answers below.

1. What was Oskar Speck's occupation when he was living in Germany? _____

2. How many people did his business employ by 1932? _____

3. From what was Germany still recovering in 1932? (two things) _____

4. What did the Great Depression force Oskar to do? _____

5. What unusual vessel did Oskar take with him on his 50 000 kilomertre journey?

   _____

6. How long did his journey take him? _____

7. What was the name of Oskar's kayak?_____

8. In which country's copper mines did he hope to find work? _____

9. In which sea is Cyprus? _____

10. List 5 countries through which Oskar travelled. _____

    _____

11. In which country did his wanderings come to an end? _____

12. What did the Indonesian tribesmen do to Oskar? _____

13. What surprising news did he learn when he reached New Guinea? _____

14. What did Australian authorities think Oskar was? _____

15. What did the authorities do with him? _____

16. Whereabouts in Australia did Oskar decide to live (state and town). _____

    _____

17. What skill did he learn there? _____

18. What did he become when he moved to Sydney? _____

19. In which year did World War Two finish? _____ ?

20. Where can you see a display of items associated with Oskar's remarkable journey?

_____

B. Find words with these meanings in the text. Some letters are given.

1. Willing to try new things, especially to make money __ __ t __ __ __ __ __ s __ __ __

2. place to which someone is travelling __ __ s __ __ __ __ t __ __ __

3. first __ n __ t __ __ __

4. made roughly, not to last __ __ k __ __ h __ f __

5. in addition, as well __ u __ __ __ __ __ m __ __ __

6. the act of putting someone in prison without
officially accusing them of a crime __ __ t __ __ n __ __ __ t

ACTIVITY – VOCABULARY

Oskar Speck had a love for adventure. Perhaps, when he was a boy he would daydream as he looked at an atlas and think to himself, ' I wonder what it's like there. 'The names in the word bank are alternative place names. Some stir the sense of wonder. Use a search engine to find their alternative names then write the words on the lines provided. The highlighted letters spell the answers to complete the information about Lake Cadibarrawirracanna.

> **Eternal   Windy City   Rising Sun   Teardrop   Square Mile   Big
> Lusitania   Canals   Huns   Apple   Skeleton   Tinsel Town   Motown
> Emerald   Holy   Cloud   O'Groats   Subcontinent   Hibernia**

1. London is sometimes called 'The __ __ __ __ __ __   __ __ __ __ __'.

2. 'The __ __ __ __ __ __ __ __ of India 'is another name for Sri Lanka.

3. Ireland is also called 'The __ __ __ __ __ __ __ Isle 'because of its beautiful green countryside.

4. Rome is also referred to as 'The __ __ __ __ __ __ __ City'.

5. 'John __ ' __ __ __ __ __ __ 'is the name of the Scottish village generally regarded as having the most northerly point on the island of Great Britain. This is disputed by some.

6. New Zealand is also known as 'The Land Of The Long White __ __ __ __ __'.

7. New York is also known as 'The Big __ __ __ __ __'.

8. Because it is a centre of the motor car industry, Detroit is also known as '__ __ __ __ __ __'.

9. Venice in Italy is known as 'The City Of __ __ __ __ __ __'. See if you can find out why.

10. Hollywood in California, USA, is sometimes called __ __ __ __ __ __ __ __ __ __.

11. __ __ __ __ __ __ __ __ __ is an old name for Portugal.

12. New Orleans in USA is also known as 'The __ __ __ Easy'.

13. Jerusalem is also called 'The __ __ __ __ City'.

14. Hungary is also known as The Land Of The __ __ __ __ .

15. Chicago in the USA is also called 'The __ __ __ __ __ City'.

16. __ __ __ __ __ __ __ is the old name for the island of Ireland.

17. India is also called 'The __ __ __ __ __ __ __ __ __ __ __'.

18. Shipwrecked sailors on the coast of Namibia usually died of thirst because the region is so dry. This region is often called 'The __ __ __ __ __ __ __ Coast'.

19. Japan is also known as 'The Land Of The __ __ __ __ __ __ __ __ __'.

Lake Cadibarrawirracanna in the South Australian desert boasts Australia's longest place name. The name means __ in the local aboriginal language.

INDICATORS AND OUTCOMES

a. answers literal questions

b. can use context to find out the meaning of words

8. THE HOLDEN STORY

The English town of Walsall in the county of Staffordshire had already been a famous centre of leatherworking for hundreds of years when James Alexander Holden was born there in 1836. James grew up in the family business, the making and repairing of leather harness and the repair of carriages and wagons.

James was a restless and ambitious teenager. He did not get on well with his stepmother. In 1852 , aged only sixteen, he decided to take a chance at making his fortune in America . He was moderately successful but still only twenty when, in 1856, he migrated again.

This time he chose the emerging town of Adelaide in the colony of South Australia. Adelaide too, was only twenty years old. European settlement had begun there in 1836.

In a weatherboard house James made and repaired leather saddles and harness and sold assorted other leather goods and ironmongery (the old word for hardware).

His reputation as a skilful craftsman saw the business soon begin to prosper. He had to move to a larger premises in Adelaide's Hindley Street.

As Adelaide grew it began to attract a wealthy class of squatters (farmers) and business people. James decided that it would be in his best interests to concentrate on the lucrative business of making coach bodies and fittings to serve these wealthy clients.

His judgment was good and the business continued to grow and employ more staff. It moved again in 1878. The new premises, in Adelaide's Grenfell Street, was to be the home of the business for more than forty years. A large wooden horse stood over its main entrance. It was to remain a well-known landmark to generations of Adelaide's citizens.

In 1885 Holden took on a business partner, the German born Henry Adolf Frost. For many years the company took on the name of Holden and Frost. James Holden died in 1887. The tiny saddler's shop had grown into a large, flourishing business during his lifetime but it was to continue its growth.

James' son, Henry, born in 1859, took over the role of his deceased father. The company grew and prospered steadily until 1899. In that year a conflict known as the *Boer War (1899–1902) began in South Africa. The Australian colonies were expected to lend assistance to England in this war against the Dutch colonialist Boers. They did not disappoint.

Holden's company was given a contract to make 10 000 sets of saddles and harness for the use of Australian mounted soldiers in this conflict. To do this work Henry Holden rented a huge shed in the Adelaide suburb of Norwood. Rows of sewing machines on trestles were set up, seemingly overnight. An army of women was recruited to do the work. The speed and efficiency with which it was done drew praise from government and military officials. The company name came to be regarded as a by-word for quality.

Henry Holden went on to become mayor of Norwood and helped establish Adelaide's tram system.

In the first decade of the 20th century Henry Holden saw the potential of the horseless carriage or motor car. Henry's youngest son, Edward, who had joined the firm in 1905 after graduating from university believed that the future lay entirely with the automobile.

Many people thought that this mode of transport would never be anything more than a rich person's plaything. How wrong they were. By the time World War I began, in 1914, it was clear that Henry and Edward were right.

Holden and Frost turned to making car bodies for the large American producers, Ford and Dodge. By 1921 the business was well established and making more than 10 000 car bodies a year.

In 1923 the company acquired a huge factory site at Woodville in Adelaide.

On his father's death in 1926, Edward became the company's chairman. He oversaw the Holden company's merger with the giant American company of General Motors. This formed the partnership known as General Motors Holden.

Edward's dream was to see Holden cars, made in Australia and running on Australian roads. Sadly, he died in 1947, one year before cars bearing the name Holden were seen on Australia's roads. The tiny saddlery started by James Holden had, in three generations, grown into one of Australia's largest and best known companies.   *(Boer is Dutch for farmer.)

Comprehension

A. Write short answers below.

1. In which county and country is the town of Walsall? _____

2. For which craft has Walsall long been well-known? _____

3. Who was born there in 1836? _____

4. What was the family business? _____

5. Why did James decide to try to make his fortune in America (3 reasons)?

_____

6. To which growing town did James migrate? _____

7. How old was James when he migrated there? _____

8. What do we mostly call ironmongery nowadays? _____

9. Why did James' business grow so quickly? _____

10. In which street in Adelaide did he move into a larger premises? _____

11. What did he concentrate on making (2 things) to satisfy the needs of wealthy customers? _____

12. To which Adelaide street did James move his business in 1878? _____

13. For how long was the business conducted from this address? _____

14. What stood over its main entrance during much of this time? _____

15. Who became James' business partner in 1885? _____

16. From which country did this man come? _____

17. In which year did James Holden die? _____

18. In which year was Henry Holden born? _____

19. In which war was Australia involved from 1899 to 1902? _____

20. What does the Dutch word Boer mean in English? _____

21. In which country was the Boer War fought? _____

22. What was Henry's company given the contract to make to help fight this war?

_____

23. In which Adelaide suburb did Henry quickly set up a factory to make the saddles and harness? _____

24. What expression does the writer use to tell you that the setting up of the factory was done very quickly? _____

25. To which high-ranking position in the suburb of Norwood did Henry Holden rise?

_____

26. What name was given to the first cars? _____

27. What did Edward, Henry's youngest son, believe was the transportation vehicle of the future? _____

28. For which large American companies did Holden and Frost make car bodies?

_____

29. To which Adelaide suburb did the company move in 1923? _____

30. In which year did the first Holden cars run on Australian roads? _____

INDICATORS AND OUTCOMES	**a.** answers literal questions makes inferences (question 9)analyses information and seeks solutions(question 30)

Activity

The words in the word bank all have something to do with cars. Some stir the sense of wonder. Use an online dictionary to check meanings then write the words on the lines provided. The highlighted letters spell the early name given to motor car engines

headlights	trunk	automatic	fender	jack	horn	panel	bio	Steamer

rear convertible reverse blinkers licence bonnet speedometer

accelerator manual dipstick seatbelt global carriage traffic brakes

1. A car with a top that can be pulled back is called a __ __ __ __ __ __ __ __ __ __ __.

2. A bumper bar is called a __ __ __ __ __ __ in USA.

3. The Stanley __ __ __ __ __ __ __ was a famous steam driven car.

4. A __ __ __ __ __ __ __ __ __ __ tells you how fast your car is travelling.

5. __ __ __ __ __ are used to slow down or stop your car.

6. The boot of a car is called the __ __ __ __ __ in USA.

7. A __ __ __ __ is used to lift a car from the ground if a tyre needs to be changed.

8. A __ __ __ __ __ __ __ __ holds you in your seat in the case of an accident.

9. A __ __ __ __ __ __ __ is a document that gives a driver permission to drive.

10. The abbreviation GPS stands for __ __ __ __ __ __ Positioning System.

11. A car with an __ __ __ __ __ __ __ __ __ transmission changes gears automatically.

12. __ __ __ fuels are fuels like ethanol that are derived from renewable resources rather than fossil fuels.

13. The driver must change the gears of a car with a __ __ __ __ __ __ transmission (as opposed to an automatic transmission).

14. If you are driving in __ __ __ __ __ __ __ you are going backwards.

15. Vehicles travelling on a road are called __ __ __ __ __ __ __ __.

16. An early name for a car was a horseless __ __ __ __ __ __ __ __ __.

17. An __ __ __ __ __ __ __ __ __ __ __ is a pedal that controls the speed of a car.

18. A car __ __ __ __ makes a loud noise to warn others of its approach.

19. A __ __ __ __ __ vision mirror allows drivers to see what is behind their vehicle.

20. The hood of a car is called the __ __ __ __ __ __ in USA.

21. __ __ __ __ __ __ __ __ __ allow drivers to see the road ahead at night time.

22. A __ __ __ __ __ __ __ __ measures the depth of oil in a car.

23. Indicators are also called __ __ __ __ __ __ __ __.

24. If your car's body has bumps in it you can take it to a __ __ __ __ __ beater to be fixed.

PUZZLE

A car's motor is called an

__ __ __ __ __ __ __ __   __ __ __ __ __ __ __ __ __   __ __ __ __

9. GEORGE PENCHEFF – PIONEER WRESTLER

If anyone showed, at an early age what they were going to be when they were an adult, it was George Pencheff. George grew up on a small farm close to a village in Russia. His father was a mountain of a man who added to his modest income from the farm by taking part in the villagers' weekend entertainment — wrestling. The local rules were simple. Anyone could challenge the champion. But there was no changing your mind once you were in the ring. The way you left the ring was by being thrown out by the victor. One weekend evening in 1923 thirteen year old George and his father were enjoying the entertainment as spectators. The current champion was a large, powerful Turkish shepherd When challengers were called for, the already strongly built George began pulling off his shirt. He was about to jump into the ring when his mother grabbed hold of his shirt and begged her husband to prevent the boy from entering the ring.

Working in the fields with George every day, he knew how strong the boy was. To appease his wife, Pencheff senior said, ' Your mother is right.' At the same time he pushed George into the ring. It took young George less than 30 seconds to send the shepherd flying through the air and out of the ring. Mother, father and son were very pleased when they received the winner's prize — a baby bull.

This bout was the first of more than 5 000 that George would have. Of these, he lost only 28 — or about one in every two hundred.

By the time George came to Australia, in 1927, his father was already well-known for feats of great strength. One of these was lifting a car and 25 men together. George's earliest days in Australia were spent in Mildura where he had heard that there was plenty of farm work available for strong, willing workers.

His first job involved clearing an area of 107 acres (43 hectares) of trees and scrub. His foreman was amazed when this was done in just three days. Work in Mildura proved to be more scarce than George had expected so he decided that he would do the job that he was known for in his home country — wrestling.

His first match was with Roy McKinnon, the local idol. George won this bout in a few seconds. Filled, now, with self-belief, he began to realize that by making himself well-known he could make a living from his favoured sport.

He approached Lew Laconeo, the leading promoter of wrestling events in Australia at the time. George was still only a teenager weighing just 75 kilograms. This was very small by wrestling standards. Laconeo waved him away and told him to come back when he was 'grown up'. 'Try me,' said George. The infuriated promoter grabbed him in a wrestling hold and a few seconds later was nursing a broken arm. Now taken seriously, George was inundated with offers from promoters wanting to promote him in wrestling bouts. He won his Australian bouts so easily that it was decided to travel the world and take on the biggest and the best.

He did this and, on average won 199 out of every 200 bouts. He wrestled against such stars as King Kong from Singapore, the highly regarded South Africans, Don Koloff and Johaness Vanderwalt and the world champion, America's Jim Londos.

In one of his bouts with Londos the world champion put George into a painful hold for two hours. The bout was declared a draw. Londos held George's arm in the air — a mark of respect that he was never to repeat with another wrestler.

George said that the greatest thrill of his life was when he wrestled before an excited audience of 140 000 to secure the Indian championship. When he won, the enthusiastic fans rushed him and many kissed the feet of the man they referred to as the **Russian Rocket.**

George retired from wrestling in the early 1960s. Even in retirement he continued a training schedule that kept him looking much younger than his true age.

COMPREHENSION

A. Write short answers below.

1. In which country did George grow up?_____

2. What was the weekend entertainment in George's village? _____

3. How did losers leave the ring in the village wrestling matches? _____

4. Whom did George defeat in his first village wrestling match? _____

5. How old was George when he had his first wrestling match? _____

6. How long did this first bout last? _____

7. What prize did the family win as a result of George's victory?_____

8. Approximately how many wrestling matches did George have altogether?

_____

9. How many of these did he lose? _____

10. When did George come to Australia? _____

11. What feat of strength did his father once perform?_____

12. Where were George's first days in Australia spent? _____

13. How long did it take George to clear 43 hectares of trees? _____

14. Who was George's first Australian opponent? _____

15. Who was the leading Australian wrestling promoter in the 1920s? _____

16. What injury did the promoter sustain after grabbing George in a wrestling hold?

_____

17. Name four prominent wrestlers of George's era? _____

18. For how long did Jim Londos hold George in a painful wrestling hold? _____

19. What did Londos do to show his respect for George after their drawn bout?

_____

20. What did George say was his biggest thrill in wrestling? _____

21. What did George's Indian fans call him? _____

22. How did some Indian fans show their admiration for George? _____

23. When did George retire from wrestling? _____

24. Assuming George was 'body slammed 'an average of twice per wrestling bout, how many 'body slams 'would he have received in his career? _____

B. What is meant by *His father was a mountain of a man*?

_____

_____

C. Write words with these meanings in the text. Some letters are given.

1. small or humble __ __ __ e __ t

2. winner __ __ c __ o __

3. strong __ __ w __ __ __ u __

4. a wrestling match __ __ u __

GEORGE PENCHEFF — PIONEER WRESTLER   ENRICHMENT

1. Wrestling is one of the oldest sports. List eight other sports that do not involve the use of a ball.

_____

2. Now list eight games that require a ball.

_____

_____

3. What is meant by a *contact* sport?

_____

_____

4. What is your favourite sport? Tell why it is your favourite.

_____

_____

5. Who is your favourite sportsperson? Give reasons.

_____

_____

6. Use the internet to research one of these well-known wrestlers. Write a short biography of the wrestler you choose. Draw a portrait underneath your information.

Hulk Hogan   Andre The Giant   The Swedish Angel   Brute Bernard
Pepper Gomez   John Cena   Gorgeous George Wagner   Antonio Inoki
Chief Little Wolf   Killer Kowalski

_____

_____

_____

_____

_____

_____

_____

7. See if you can find video footage of some bouts. Write which bout is your favourite. Don't copy anything you see without permission from a parent or guardian.

INDICATORS AND OUTCOMES	
	a. answers literal questions
	b. recognises imagery and is aware of its use as a literary device
	c. can use context to find out the meaning of words

10. THE PRIME MINISTER WHO LOVED THE SEA

The morning of Sunday, 17th December, 1967 was overcast but warm in Melbourne. Things were winding down for the Christmas holiday period. Harold Holt, Australia's popular Prime Minister at the time, went with some friends to a good vantage point to watch round-the-world-sailor, Alec Rose, enter Port Phillip Bay in his yawl named the *Lively Lady*.

Having done this the group moved on in two cars to one of the Prime Minister's favourite swimming spots — the nearby Cheviot Beach. This beach takes its name from the passenger steamer, the Cheviot, which was wrecked there eighty years earlier with the loss of 35 lives.

Holt had taken up snorkelling in 1954. He said that it was the perfect way for him to counter the pressures of public life.

At around midday he moved ahead of the group walking along the sand dunes. In his swimming trunks and sandshoes he entered the water. An experienced snorkeler and swimmer, he had earlier declared to his companions, ' I know this beach like the back of my hand.

He quickly swam out about sixty metres. His friend, Alan Stewart, followed but decided that the water was too rough. He went back onto the beach where he joined Marjorie Gillespie, another of the group of friends. Moments later Mrs Gillespie began to be concerned for the Prime Minister's safety and shouted for him to come back onto the shore. But the roaring waters drowned out her calls.

'I saw that Harold was still swimming but he seemed to be getting farther away all the time and I felt very strongly that all was not well,' she told investigating police. Describing his disappearance she said, ' I watched continuously and the water became turbulent around him very suddenly and seemed to boil. These conditions seemed to swamp on him. It was like a leaf being taken out. It was so quick and final. '

Mr Stewart ran to his car and reported the disappearance at the Army Officer Cadet School at Portsea, about five kilometres away. From here he contacted the police who officially began their search at 1.56 p.m.

An exhaustive search involving eight helicopters and three hundred searchers found no trace of the missing Prime Minister. The sudden disappearance of this popular Prime Minister after only 696 days in office left the nation in shock. Sir John McKewen was sworn in as the caretaker Prime Minister until Mr Holt's party colleagues chose someone to replace him. Among those who attended his funeral was Lyndon Baines Johnson, the President of the United States of America, who had developed a good friendship and understanding with Mr Holt. In a show of support for the President Mr Holt once said that he hoped, ' …that there will be a corner of your mind and heart which takes cheer from the fact that you have an admiring friend, a staunch friend, that will be all the way with L B J.'

Following the disappearance all sorts of strange and outlandish conspiracy theories were aired. One was that Mr Holt had been spying on Australia for China and had been whisked back to there in a submarine. More likely, however, is that he succumbed to the rough sea and that his body may have been eaten by sharks or carried far out to sea by the strong undercurrents noted in the area. There seems little doubt that the sea that he loved so much is his final resting place.

COMPREHENSION

Write short answers below.

1. What was the date of Mr Holt's disappearance? _____

2. Who was the round-the-world sailor entering Port Phillip Bay on that day?

    _____

    _____

3. Which city is located on Port Phillip Bay? _____

4. Write the dictionary meaning of yawl.

    _____

    _____

5. What was the name of Alec Rose's yawl? _____

6. Which beach was one of Mr Holt's favourites? _____

7. From what does this beach take its name? _____

8. What leisure activity did Mr Holt take up in 1954? _____

9. What was Mr Holt wearing when he entered the water? _____

10. Had Mr Holt been to this beach before? Give a reason for your answer.

    _____

11. Why did Mr Holt probably not hear Mrs Gillespie when she called him to go back on

    shore? _____

12. What did Mrs Gillespie say the drowning was like? _____

13. Where was the disappearance first reported? _____

14. At what time did the police begin their search? _____

15. How many helicopters were involved in the search? _____

16. How many people were involved in the search? _____

17. For how many days had Mr Holt held the position of Prime Minister? _____

18. Who was given the position of caretaker Prime Minister? _____

19. Which US president attended the funeral? _____

20. What famous quote of support did Mr Holt once make to Mr Johnson?

_____

21. Why do you think Mr Johnson was also known as LBJ? _____

22. What was one far-fetched theory about Mr Holt's disappearance?

_____

23. What most likely happened to Mr Holt? _____

24. What is believed to be Mr Holt's final resting place? _____

Activity

A. Find words with these meanings in the text. Some letters are given.

1. cloudy __ __ e __ __ __ s __

2. skilful as a result of doing something numerous times __ __ p __ __ __ __ __ __ c __ __

3. worried __ __ n __ __ __ n __ __

4. well-liked __ __ __ __ __ a __

5. ceremony honouring a dead person __ __ __ __ __ a __

6. happiness __ __ __ __ __

B. Number these headlines in the order they would have appeared. One is already numbered for you.

    a. PRIME MINISTER DISAPPEARS (4   )

    b. HOLT WINS ELECTION SEAT (_____)

    c. MR HOLT MOURNED AT FUNERAL (_____)

    d. ALEC ROSE TO VISIT PORT PHILLIP TOMORROW (_____)

    e. HOLT ELECTED NEW PRIME MINISTER (_____)

    f. SIR JOHN MCKEWEN SWORN IN AS CARETAKER P.M. (_____)

C. Write a dictionary meaning of the term *conspiracy theory*.

_____

_____

D. Below is an example of a conspiracy theory.

MAN BITES DOG — ALIENS SUSPECTED

Scruffy the poodle / Alsatian cross of the wealthy businessman, Godfrey Blithers, was on the receiving end of some rough justice yesterday. Known for his surly manner, Scruffy was feared and respected but not liked by members of Mr Blithers staff. He began to growl when Mr Blithers private secretary, Muldino Metternich, began teasing him with a rubber bone. Metternich Is said to have 'snapped 'and nipped Scruffy. Both man and beast are assisting police with inquiries. Neville Sauerbraten, spokesman for the activist group, Aliens Out ! 'said that there had lately been several incidents reported to him of aliens taking control of people's minds. 'I warned you all! 'he said. 'It will get worse. They're coming, they're invisible and they're not alone!'

Now write your own conspiracy theory on the lines below.

_____

_____

_____

E. Use the internet to find and list Australia's five first Prime Ministers.

_____

_____

_____

INDICATORS AND OUTCOMES		
	a.	uses context to work out the meaning of words
	b.	can logically sequence events in a text
	c.	can use online dictionaries to find meanings of words or terms
	d.	can write an imaginative text
	e.	uses the internet as a research tool

11. PERCY GRAINGER

To many people the world of 'high art' can be intimidating. Australian pianist and composer, Percy Grainger's skills as a musician elevated the pieces he composed and played to the status of 'high art'. Grainger, however, wanted nothing to do with such stuffiness. He believed art belonged together with laughter and enjoyment. In his estimation music was joyful noise and he made it clear to everyone that this was how he regarded it.

Grainger's father was born in England and migrated to Melbourne where he married Rose Aldridge, a competent musician. Percy was born in 1882. Soon after his father, who had a love of alcohol, abandoned the family. To support herself and young Percy, Rose Grainger became a music teacher. By far her most impressive student was her gifted son, Percy.

At the age of twelve Percy gave his first public piano recital. School had never really agreed with him. His formal education lasted only three months. When he began to persistently 'wag' school his mother decided to keep him at home. Here he amused and totally absorbed himself in reading Viking myths and legends. Any other spare time was spent, practicing the piano. Probably thinking of some of the great Viking heroes as he did this, his style was described as violent and flamboyant.

To improve his technique Percy's mother took her red headed prodigy to Professor Louis Pabet, regarded as the finest teacher of piano in Australia at that time.

After two years his mother had scraped together sufficient money to take Percy to Frankfurt in Germany. Here he studied at a highly regarded conservatorium (music school). It was here that he came into the company of some very interesting characters. It was probably the most carefree time of his life.

His student days had just come to an end when his mother fell and injured herself while ice skating and was unable to continue her music teaching. Percy went to London to earn a living as a solo performer taking his mother with him as manager.

His extravagant style and wild red hair gained him some attention but, more than anything, it was the quality of his playing that won him respect. His concerts were events that were very loosely structured with Percy often ceasing to play to tell the audience some anecdotes about his life. Sometimes he would get up and push his piano to a part of the stage that he thought might result in better sound quality.

He became known as The Running Pianist because he would often run from his home to a recital. He did this, he said, because it saved him money and he enjoyed the exercise.

In 1903, on a tour of South Africa and Australia with singer, Ada Crossly, he developed whitlows (painful sores on the fingertips) on the boat trip across. These were the result of him helping the ship's stoker shovel coal for the engine. Again he said that this was done for his amusement and also for exercise.

While in South Africa, Percy insisted on walking from venue to venue rather than travelling on coaches or trains. This made his fellow artist very nervous as it would often be a matter of minutes to the scheduled starting time before Percy turned up in his trade mark pair of shorts and shirt. In spite of these distractions, the tour was a great success. In 1906 Percy met the great Norwegian composer, Edvard Grieg (best known for The Peer Gynt Suite). This meeting rekindled Percy's interest in folk songs. The next few years of his life were spent travelling from village to village in rural Britain noting down the songs sung locally before they became forgotten and lost forever. Among those he rediscovered were Danny Boy and In An English Country Garden.

Terrible tragedy entered Percy's life in 1922 when his mother ended her life jumping from the eighteenth storey of a New York building. Six years after this sad event Percy married Ella Strom, a Swedish born poet. He continued to tour and surprise his audiences. At a concert in Hobart in 1937 he played Home Sweet Home using beer bottles filled with different levels of water. He told another audience that he practiced eight hours a day on a very big piano. He told them he had such a large piano because ,' … it is handy to store dirty linen in.'

Percy continued to enthral audiences but failing health caused him to lessen his workload. He died in February, 1961, a few months after his final performance.

COMPREHENSION

A. Write short answers below.

1. Which two things did Percy Grainger believe belonged with art? (2 things)

   _____

2. What did he think music was? _____

3. Where was Percy's father born? _____

4. What was the maiden name of Percy's mother? _____

5. In which year was Percy born?_____

6. What did Percy's father have a love of ? _____

7. What did Percy's mother become to help support herself and young Percy?

   _____

8. Who was her most gifted student? _____

9. At what age did Percy give his first public recital? _____

10. How long did Percy's formal education last? _____

11. Which stories absorbed young Percy? _____

12. How did people describe his piano playing? (2 words) _____

13. What colour was Percy's hair? _____

14. To which noted piano teacher did Percy go? _____

15. In which German city did he study? _____

16. What is a music conservatorium? _____

17. What prevented Percy's mother from continuing to teach? _____

18. Where did Percy go to earn a living as a solo performer? _____

19. Who was his manager? _____

20. What unusual things did Percy often do during his concerts? (2 things)

   * _____

   * _____

21. Why was he called The Running Pianist?_____

22. Give two reasons Percy gave for running to his concerts. _____

23. What are whitlows? _____

24. What caused Percy to develop whitlows? _____

25. Which singer did Percy accompany on a 1903 tour of South Africa? _____

26. How did Percy travel from venue to venue on his South African tour?_____

27. Why did this make his fellow artists nervous? _____

28. Which famous Norwegian composer influenced Percy? _____

29. Which suite is this composer best known for? _____

30. Which famous song did Percy rediscover? _____

31. What tragedy entered Percy's life in 1922? _____

32. What reason did Percy give for playing such a big piano? _____

ACTIVITY

A. Research and put in the missing numbers.

A piano has _____ keys. There are _____ white keys and _____ black keys.

B.

1. What is ivory? _____

2. What is meant by tinkling the ivories? _____

C. Choose and highlight the person who plays each instrument.

1. A (pianoist   pianola   pianistro   pianist) plays the piano.

2. A (violist   violinist   violer   Violetta) plays the violin.

3. Someone who plays the flute is called a (flautist   fluteist   flutician   fruiterer).

4. Someone who plays the cello is called a (cellissimo   celloist   cellist   cellish).

5. A (saxophone   saxophonebone   saxephist   saxophonist) plays the saxophone.

6. Someone who plays the harp is a (harpist   harpy   harpo   harpologist).

7. A (tubist   tubaba   tubal   tubiquitist) plays the tuba.

8. Someone who plays the trumpet is a (trumpelo   trumbolist   trumpeter   trumpetist).

9. A (banji-ist   hillbilly   banjophonist   banjo player) plays the banjo.

10. Someone who plays the guitar is a (gizmo   guitarzan   guitarist   guitarphonist).

Harpist, harpy, harpo or harpologist?

D. Add the correct beginning and ending letters to complete the musical instrument names.

1. __andoli__	8. __anj__	15. __rumpe__
2. __ylophon__	9. __agpipe__	16. __orne__
3. __ymba__	10. __assoo__	17. __ioli__
4. __iol__	11. __ar__	18. __ian__
5. __armonic__	12. __ecorde__	19. __ub__
6. __ru__	13. __astane__	20. __rga__
7. __larine__	14. __iccol__	

Nero fiddles while Rome burns. What happened?

_____

_____

_____

_____

INDICATORS AND OUTCOMES

a. answers literal and inferential questions (question 4)

12. SYDNEY CUNNINGHAM, O A M THE BLACK SANTA

Sydney Arthur Cunningham loved children. He loved to see their eyes light up at Christmas time when they saw what 'Santa' had brought them. But he also knew that there were some children that Santa forgot. These were the Aboriginal children from poor families around New South Wales.

Sydney, a descendant of the Yuen Aboriginal people of the New South Wales south coast, decided to do something about it. Putting on some red overalls, a red pyjama top and gumboots, he became Santa for these needy children. The idea worked.

Sydney became Santa for thousands of children every year. In 1998, the year before he died, over 6 000 children in the Bourke, Wellington, Gilgandra and Peak Hill districts received gifts from him. He worked tirelessly seeking funds and asking for donations of toys so that the special magic of Christmas could be enjoyed by these children of poor families.

He would ring radio and television stations and appeal for donations. Even when he was retired he would set himself up for the day with a chair, table and bucket in King Street, Newtown (a suburb of Sydney). The sign on his table read: Wellington Aboriginal children. We need your help for a bush Christmas.

Peter Piggott was 'Black Santa's helper" for a number of years. He flew the helicopter in which Black Santa made his flying visits. 'He didn't want anything for himself. He just loved kids, 'Peter said of him.

Sydney spent much of his life giving to others. He served his country in the army and the air force in Papua New Guinea during World War II. During this service his health was affected by an affliction that was to be with him until his death.

Recognising his tremendous contribution to Australia, he was made 'ANZAC Of The Year 'by the Returned Soldiers' League in 1982. In 1987 he was named 'Australian Aboriginal Of The Year 'and in 1989 he was presented with the Order Of Australia Medal.

While he appreciated these awards, his greatest reward came in the happy fulfilment he saw in children's eyes after they had received a visit from Black Santa. After a lifetime of giving to the children and to his country, Sydney Cunningham passed away in his sleep at Balmain Hospital in March of 1999.

A. Write short answers below.

1.   Of which aboriginal people was Sydney a descendant? _____

2.   From which part of NSW do these people come? _____

3.   Which people did Sydney know Santa had forgotten? _____

4.   What did Sydney wear as Black Santa? _____

5.   How many children received gifts from Black Santa in 1998? _____

6.   What did Sydney do to appeal for donations? _____

7.   What were his fundraising tools in King Street, Newtown? _____

8.   What did he travel in to reach some faraway places? _____

9.   Where did Sydney serve during World War II? _____

10. Which award did he receive from the RSL in 1982? _____

11. Which award did he receive in 1987? _____

12. Which award was he given in 1989? _____

B. Find the Christmas words in the puzzle. Use different colours to colour them. One is done for you.

| TOYS | PRESENTS | GIFTS | CAROLS | CHRISTMAS TREE |
| CHRIST | NATIVITY | MAGI |

T	S	C	A	C	H	E	E	R
O	Y	S	R	I	R	N	A	T
R	P	T	O	S	T	I	T	S
E	S	F	L	M	A	V	I	A
N	E	I	S	I	G	Y	T	M
T	S	G	C	H	R	I	S	T

C. Use the internet to do a lyrics search for the Christmas carols below. Write the missing words on the lines.

1.   God rest ye merry __ __ __ __ __ __ __ __ __

2.   Ding dong merrily on __ __ __ __

3.   Silent night, holy __ __ __ __ __

4.   The first __ __ __ __

5.   Oh come all ye __ __ __ __ __ __ __ __ __

6.   Joy to the __ __ __ __ __

7.   Away in a __ __ __ __ __ __

D. Write an ACROSTIC POEM using the letters in CHRISTMAS as the first letters of each line.

C_____

H_____

R_____

I_____

S_____

T_____

M_____

A_____

S_____

ACTIVITY– ABORIGINAL ACHIEVERS

Match the people in the word bank with what their achievements. Use the internet for research.

Archie Roach	Cathy Freeman	'Mum Shirl'	Graham 'Polly' Farmer
David Gulpilil	Ernie Dingo	Albert Namatjira	Harold Blair
Kyle Vander-Kuyp	Charles Perkins	Neville Bonner	The Ella Brothers
Mal Meninga	Eddie Mabo	Lionel Rose	David Unaipon
Oodgeroo Noonuccal		Jackey Jackey (Galmahra)	
Evonne Cawley (Goolagong)		Sir (Pastor) Douglas Nicholls	

1. Kind-hearted lady who devoted her life to being a 'Mum' to young men with troubled backgrounds. _____

2. The first Aborigine elected to Federal Parliament (in the Senate or 'Upper House'. He continued working on behalf of Aborigines after his career in politics.

   _____

3. Singer and songwriter who is best known for the song 'They Took The Children Away.' This song tells of Aboriginal children who, like him, were separated from their families at a very young age.

   _____

4. Champion athlete and footballer in his youth who became a spokesman for Aboriginal people, and later, Governor of South Australia.

   _____

5. Activist whose efforts led to the 'Mabo Law'. This law put an end to the notion that Australia was unoccupied at the time of European settlement.

   _____

6. Faithful friend of the explorer, Edmund Kennedy. He nursed his friend at the risk of great personal danger until Kennedy died . _____

7. A very gifted painter of Australian landscapes. _____

8. A renowned classical tenor (singer). _____

9. An Australian champion athlete who specialised in racing over the hurdles. _____

10. Australia's first aboriginal world boxing champion. _____

11. Author, preacher and inventor whose picture is on Australia's $50 note. _____

12. One of the all-time greats in Australian football, he played 392 senior games. _____

13. A popular actor, comedian and television presenter. _____

14. A poet and author, she won many awards for her writing which stressed the Aboriginal point of view. She was also known as Kath Walker. _____

15. An outstanding football (soccer) player who later became a political activist. He did this to draw attention to the injustices suffered by Aborigines. _____

16. Great female tennis player who won the Wimbledon title (considered the top world title) in 1971 and 1980. _____

17. Wonderful runner who has represented Australia at Olympic and Commonwealth Games levels. Gold medallist in the Olympic 800 metre race in 2000. _____

18. Formerly a policeman, this outstanding rugby league player captained Australia on many occasions. Represented Queensland in 32 State Of Origin games. _____

19. An actor and traditional dancer / storyteller. He has appeared in many popular films including *Crocodile Dundee* and *Storm Boy*. _____

20. Talented brothers with the names Mark, Glen and Gary who excelled at many sports but made their biggest impact playing Rugby Union for Australia. Mark captained the Australian team. _____

INDICATORS & OUTCOMES	a. answers literal questions
	b. follows written directions
	c. uses the internet as a research tool
	d. can write an acrostic poem

13. THE ANIMALS' FRIEND – LOUISA LORT SMITH

As a young girl Louisa Montgomery would drive a goat-cart around the paddocks of The Heart, her parents' farm in Victoria's Gippsland. She would look for calves that had become lost or had been abandoned by their mothers. Any that she found, she would bring back to the homestead to be cared for. She was horrified by some of the things done to animals on the farm. She saw the terror in the eyes of cattle as they were being branded. From a very young age she made up her mind to do everything she could to stop cruelty to animals.

When she grew up Louisa married Charles Lort Smith, a prominent Melbourne solicitor. Because her husband's work often involved overseas travel, Louisa took note of how animals were treated in other places. Things that she thought were beneficial she proposed to authorities in Melbourne when she returned there.

While travelling in Britain in 1929 she visited an animal clinic to which poor people could take their sick pets. Here, any medical problems the animals had could be treated for free. When she returned to Australia she proposed that this should be done in Melbourne. She approached the Chancellor of Melbourne University, who allowed her to use a veterinary school in the suburb of Parkville. The news of this spread rapidly and 4 000 cases were treated in the first year. An ambulance was donated so the animals of sick or elderly people who were unable to walk could be picked up and transported to the hospital.

While she was popular with animal lovers, there were some people who regarded her as a nuisance. If she saw cruelty being visited upon an animal she would confront those responsible, exposing and embarrassing them. Even if she was dealing with powerful people she would not be silenced.

Louisa was highly critical of the manner in which animals were displayed at Melbourne Zoo. Her very public criticisms played a large part in having the displays rebuilt in such a way that the animals were more humanely housed.

Her longest and most gruesome battle was with the Melbourne City Council regarding practices at the city abattoirs. She wrote to newspapers and spoke at public meetings, telling, quite graphically of the cruel methods that were in use there. In 1949 the then Victorian Premier, John Cain, enacted laws that saw many of her suggestions being put into action. Louisa said she had spoken up for animals because they were unable to speak up for themselves. ' I'll go on championing the cause of Victoria's animals until I die, but don't make me out to be a crank, ' she told a reporter. ' People seem to think you are a crank if you want to see animals treated decently. '

Louisa Lort Smith died 1n 1956, but the work of the Lort Smith animal hospital goes on. In 2000 the hospital moved to a larger, more modern building. Thirty vets and forty nurses are employed there. Since opening in 1936, the hospital (up until 2012) has cared for over five million animals and found homes for more than two hundred thousand of them.

A. Write short answers below.

1. What was Louisa looking for as she drove around her parents' farm in a goat-cart?
_____

2. What was the name of Louisa's husband?_____

3. What did Louisa take particular notice of when she travelled overseas
_____

4. How many animals were treated for free at Parkville Veterinary School in its first year helping poor animal owners? _____

5. What was donated to transport sick animals or their elderly owners?
_____

6. How did Louisa improve things for animals at Melbourne Zoo? _____

7. What reason did Louisa give for speaking up for animals? _____

8. How many animals had her hospital cared for from 1936 to 2012?_____

B. Highlight the quote that you think best suits Louisa's attitude to life?

1. A fool and his money are soon parted. _____

2. A rolling stone gathers no moss. _____

3. Half a loaf is better than no bread at all. _____

4. The good person is the friend of all animals. _____

5. Don't cry over spilt milk._____

6. Don't count your chickens before they are hatched. _____

7. Highlight five words that could be used to describe Louisa Lort Smith.

_____

silly	generous	avaricious	greedy	stingy	caring
grasping	determined	kind	cruel	persistent	miserly

C.]Find words in the text with the meanings given. Some letters are given.

1. well-known __ __ __ m __ __ __ __ n __

2. suggested __ r __ __ __ s __ __

3. kindly or sympathetically __ u __ __ __ __ __ l __

4. passed a law __ n __ c __ __ __ __

5. in a very clear and detailed manner; giving a good picture __ __ __ p __ __ c __ __ __ __ __

D. What am I? I am an animal. I eat plants. My skin is grey and thick. I can spray you with water. My nose is called a trunk. I have tusks made of ivory. What am I?

You are _____.

Now write your own animal What Am I? Write at least four clues.

_____

_____

ACTIVITY

The animals in the word bank are sometimes coupled with some words in the sentences below. Match them with their partners in the activity. Highlighted letters spell out the answers to the riddles. Put them in the spaces in the order they occur to solve the riddles.

> dove monkey tiger wolf rabbit hare goat crocodile hawk eagle pony zebra kiwi cat fox horse worm turtle lion spider crab beetle snake sheep canary loan kangaroo spider donkey bee duck

Riddle 1: I am at the beginning of the end and the end of time and space. I am essential to creation and I surround every place. What am I?

__ __ __ __   __ __ __ __ __ __ __ __   __ __

1. A person or thing that appears powerful and dangerous but that is actually weak and ineffectual is sometimes called a paper __ __ __ __ __.

2. A warlike person can be called a __ __ __ __ __.

3. A __ __ __ __ __ __ __ wrench is a type of adjustable spanner.

4. To eat food ravenously without chewing is to __ __ __ __ __ it down.

5. Someone with excellent vision can be described as being __ __ __ __ __ eyed

6. An indoor, V shaped television antenna can be called __ __ __ __ __ __ ears.

number 6

7. A __ __ __ __ee is a small chin beard that is trimmed to a point.

8. People who cry falsely or pretend sorrow are said to shed __ __ __ __ __ __ __ __ __ __ tears.

9. A __ __ __ __ brained idea is one that is silly.

10. A peaceful person is sometimes referred to as a __ __ __ __.

Riddle 2: I am a green house. Inside the green house is a white house. Inside the white house there is a red house. In the red house are many babies. What am I? __   __ __ __ __ __ __ __ __ __ __ __ __

11. A __ __ __ __ -of-nine tails is a whip with nine knotted cords.

12. The Chinese gooseberry is also called the __ __ __ __ fruit.

13. A __ __ __ __ apple is a small, sour apple.

14. What we call a skivvy in Australia and a polo neck jumper in UK the Americans call a __ __ __ __ __ __ neck sweater.

15. Pedestrians are able to cross the road safely at a __ __ __ __ __ crossing.

16. __ __ __ __ __ __ power is used to measure the power of mechanical engines.

17. A book __ __ __ __ is someone who loves reading books.

18. A __ __ __ __ __ __ monkey has extremely long, thin arms and legs.

19. Because he was fearless in battle, Richard 1 of England was caled Richard the __ __ __ __ hearted.

20. The __ __ __ trot is a dance.

21. A __ __ __ __ tail is a hairstyle in which the hair is pulled back and tied at the back of the head.

Riddle 3: *Which word in the English language has three consecutive double letters?* __ __ __ __ __ __ __ __ __ __

22. A water boatman is a type of __ __ __ __ __ __.

23. A __ __ __ __ shark lends money at exorbitant interest (often for illegal purposes.

24. A __ __ __ __ __ __ __ __ court is an unofficial court made up of people wanting to try someone and find them guilty without the good evidence required from a proper court.

25. Someone who makes outlandish, unproven claims about goods they are selling (especially for medicinal purposes) may be called a __ __ __ __ __ oil salesman.

26. Someone who scores no runs in a cricket innings is said to have made a __ __ __ __.

27. A __ __ __ line is the shortest straight line to something.

28. A __ __ __ __ __ __ engine is a small steam engine, often on board a ship.

29. __ __ __ __ __ __ veins are narrow blood vessels which radiate in a network, often on the nose or legs.

30. A black __ __ __ __ __ is someone who is not looked upon favourably in their family because of their disreputable behaviour. __ __ __ __ __ __ yellow is a very bright yellow colour.

INDICATORS & OUTCOMES	**a.** answers literal questions
	b. understands the main idea of a text
	c. recognises different character types and traits
	d. uses context to work out the meaning of words (E) can write a simple description

14. LES DARCY

The 'big three' of Australian sport are generally acknowledged to be the world's greatest ever cricketer, Don Bradman, the mighty racehorse Phar Lap, known as the Red Terror, and a handsome, slow talking boy from Maitland, New South Wales — Les Darcy.

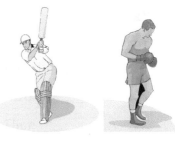

On 30th September, 1916 some 12 000 people packed into the Sydney Stadium, the home of boxing in New South Wales, and saw the young man from Maitland knock out the former world champion, George Chip. In his preceding 49 fights Darcy had won 44, lost 4 and drawn one. His victory against the former world champion saw him approaching the peak of his career. But tragic events unfolded in his life and the victory against Chip was to be the 21 year old's last fight.

Born near Maitland, New South Wales, in 1895, the strongly built boy took up the task of being a blacksmith's striker at the age of 16. The striker was a blacksmith's apprentice whose job it was to swing the heavy sledgehammer in large forging operations. Amazed by his tremendous strength, few people were surprised when Les took up boxing to make a little money on the side. With Mick Hawkins, a Maitland gymnasium owner as his trainer and manager, Les fought a number of professional bouts in Newcastle before stepping up to the 'big time' at the famous Sydney Stadium.

With ferocious punching power he won a string of fights from 1914 to 1916 and was so impressive that he was spoken of as the next world champion in the middleweight division. When he defeated Chip he made arrangements to travel to America to take on Al McCoy, holder of the world middleweight title. But these plans turned out to be not so easy to fulfil. Australia was engaged in World War I and the issue of conscription (compulsory military service) was dividing the country.

Les had not enlisted and was criticised by some as a shirker. His answer to these accusers was that he had tried to enlist twice but was rejected because he was under twenty-one years of age and his parents had refused to give him their consent.

The War Precautions Act did not allow any able bodied man between the ages of 17 and 45 to leave Australia. Les pleaded with government officials to allow him to go to the United States and spend enough time there to have a title fight with McCoy. Frustrated by constant refusal he and his new manager, Tim Sullivan, decided to stow away on an American freighter. With Les and Sullivan hiding in its hold the vessel sailed on the night of 26th October, 1916. By the time they were discovered by crew members it was too late to turn the ship around and put back to Australia.

The ship let them off at a port in Chile and from there they took passage to New York.

Les's reputation preceded him and, at first, he was well received in New York. Within a few days fight promoter, Tex Rickard announced plans for a title bout between the young Australian and Al McCoy, the reigning world champion. Meanwhile reporters began asking Les about his secretive departure from Australia and why he hadn't volunteered for the armed forces. In Australia his reputation was in tatters. He was denounced and stripped of his Australian heavyweight and middleweight titles and the fight with Al McCoy was cancelled. He was banned from boxing in New York and several other states.

America entered World War I on 6th April, 1917. Three weeks later Les collapsed and was rushed to hospital. He had developed septicaemia from two infected teeth. His tonsils were removed but he developed pneumonia and on May 24th, 1917 the golden boy of Australian boxing was dead. His fiancé, Winnie O'Sullivan, was at his bedside.

After a huge funeral in San Francisco Les's body was returned to Australia for another enormous funeral. By the time of his burial in the Catholic section of East Maitland cemetery he had regained his status as a national hero.

COMPREHENSION

A. Write short answers below.

1. List the big three of Australian sport. _____

2. Where was Les born? _____

3. What was Les's job? _____

4. Les had two managers during his career. Who were they? _____

5. In which weight division did Les fight? _____

6. Who was the world champion in this division? _____

7. Write the dictionary definition of conscription. _____
    _____

8. Why did some people say that Les was a shirker? _____

9. What reason did Les give for not enlisting in the army? (Give two parts to your answer.) _____

10. Which act did not allow men aged between 17 and 45 to leave Australia?
    _____

11. What caused Les to get septicaemia? _____

12. What was the name of Les's fiancé? _____

B. ADJECTIVES are DESCRIBING WORDS. They describe things. They usually stand immediately before the things they describe. E.g. a powerful man; powerful is the adjective. It tells what sort of man. Find the adjectives to describe each thing below. The words can be found in the text. Some letters are given.

1. Phar Lap __ __ g __ __ __

2. Les __ __ __ __ s __ m __

3. Les's strength __ __ __ m __ __ d __ __ __

4. Les's funeral __ __ o __ m __ __ __

C. Skim the text and find these words. Write them in the order they occur.

Chile	pneumonia	national	shirker

_____

_____

D. Find words with these meanings in the text. Some letters are given.

1. nearing __ __ __ __ __ a c __ __ __ __ __

2. hide on a ship __ __ __ __ a __ a __

3. person who avoids work __ __ __ __ __ e __

4. healthy __ __ __ e __ o __ __ __ d

ACTIVITY

A. Boxing bouts are organised according to weights. Fighters are placed into various weight divisions so they are competing against opponents of similar size. Match the fighting divisions with their weight limits. Note that there are other weight divisions. Those listed in the word bank are the 'traditional' (older) divisions. Use the internet to do your research.

Lightweight	Light Heavyweight	Flyweight	Heavyweight
Cruiserweight	Bantamweight	Middleweight	Welterweight
	Featherweight		

Weight Division	Division Weight Limit
_____	Unlimited
_____	90.7 kg
_____	79.4 kg
_____	72.5 kg
_____	66.7 kg
_____	61.2 kg
_____	57.2 kg
_____	53.5 kg
_____	50.8 kg

B. What are the Marquess of Queensberry Rules?

_____

_____

_____

C. What does the term 'punch drunk' mean?

_____

_____

_____

D. YOUR POINT OF VIEW

Should boxing be banned? Do the benefits of boxing (such as the discipline of training and physical fitness) outweigh the dangers (such as brain concussion from repeated blows to the head). What do you think? Give at least three reasons that support your point of view.

_____

_____

_____

_____

_____

_____

_____

_____

_____

_____

INDICATORS & **OUTCOMES**	**a.** answers literal questions
	b. identifies grammatical features in a text
	c. locates information by skimming
	d. uses context to work out the meaning of words

Scientists are often portrayed in books and films as absent-minded people so distracted by their latest invention or theory that they become figures of fun. The reality, however, is generally far from this. While their work is seldom spectacular or extravagant, it is responsible for improving people's everyday lives.

Doctor George Bornemissza came to Australia from the country of his birth, Hungary, in 1950. He had studied to become an entomologist, a scientist specialising in the study of insects. The work of the entomologist involves the collecting of specimens outdoors. As Doctor Bornemissza did his field work he noticed the large number of cowpats on farmland. One cow can produce close to a dozen pats a day. With almost twice as many cows in Australia as people, this created problems.

To cows there is a ring of repugnance around every cowpat. If you look at a cowpat in a paddock the grass next to it is usually longer than grass growing further away. Cows avoid eating grass close to a cowpat leading to a reduction in the amount of productive pasture land. The pats are also favoured breeding spots for flies. They lay their eggs in the cowpats and the manure provides food for their grubs. These flies do tremendous damage, especially to sheep.

Doctor Bornemissza knew that in his former homeland and in other parts of the world, there was no such problem. Cowpats in these places were quickly dispersed and buried by dung beetles. Like flies, these beetles lay their eggs in dung. Their habits, however, are different.

They break off a piece of dung (1), roll it into a ball (2), lay an egg in the ball (3) and bury it.

1.

2.

3.

When the egg hatches the larva has a ready supply of food.

Australia has its native dung beetles but they lay their eggs in the small, hard droppings of our native animals and ignore those of introduced animals like cattle and sheep. Doctor Bornemissza suggested that beetles be imported to clean up cowpats in Australia.

From 1967 to 1970 various species were collected from other countries and trialled in Australia. The trials proved successful. Importantly, this method of fly control did not involve the use of deadly pesticides which can find their way into the food chain.

Thanks to the dedicated work of Doctor Bornemissza and his team, Australia's pastures have increased in size. The incidence of such fatal ailments as blowfly strike in sheep has also been reduced.

1.

    a. Doctor Bornemissza worked for the CSIRO. What do the initials CSIRO stand for?

_____

    b. How many legs does an adult insect have? _____

    c. Name three different members of the beetle family. _____

_____

    d. What is the capital city of Hungary? _____ _____

    e. Name two different types of flies _____

    f. Who and what were The Beatles?_____

2. Choose from the words in the word bank to match the things they study. Colour each word in the word bank as you use it.

> **entomology   geology   astronomy   biology   bacteriology   ornithology
> botany   meteorology   pharmacology   geometry   geography   zoology
> anatomy   archaeology**

    a. _____ is the study of ancient civilisations. It often involves the digging up the ruins of these civilisations.

    b. _____ is the study of animals.

    c. _____ is the study of the structure of bodies of living things.

    d. _____ is the study of is the study of living things.

    e. _____ is the study of rocks.

    f. _____ is the study of the weather.

    g. _____ is the study of the stars and planets.

    h. _____ is the study of plants.

    i. _____ is the study of the Earth's surface.

    j. _____ is the study of insects.

    k. _____ is the study of birds.

    l. _____ is the study of shapes, lines and curves.

    m. _____ is the study of germs.

    n. _____ is the study of drugs and medicines.

3. Make up some of your own ' –ologies' e.g. GARBOLOGY – the study of GARBAGE.

_____

BIOLOGICAL CONTROL

Like other animals, humans must compete for the food the world provides. By farming the way we do, we make conditions ideal for certain creatures to build up large populations. Because these creatures eat food we like and make it unfit for us to eat, we regard them as pests and devise methods to control their numbers. A common method used to control pests is through the use of poisons. Unfortunately, these poisons often affect not only the pests but other helpful creatures as well. These poisons are made to kill living things, and people are living things. Many poisons stay in the soil for a very long time and enter the water supply and food chain.

FOOD CHAIN:

A bee gathering nectar enters a sprayed orchard. It becomes affected by the poison while on the wing and falls into a creek where a fish eats it. (Sometimes poison leaches through the soil into waterways). Fish eat insects affected by spray in the orchard, so poison builds up in their bodies. The fish is eaten by humans who also eat the poison.

1. -> 2. 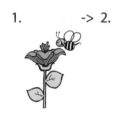  -> 3.  -> 4.

A safer way to control pests is to find creatures that feed on them. This is called biological control, and must be done with great care. In 1935 the cane toad was introduced from South America to the sugar cane fields of Queensland. It was supposed to control beetles that ruined the cane. It failed to do this and has become a pest itself because it has no natural enemies here. In 1859 Thomas Austin released 24 wild English rabbits on his farm near Geelong in Victoria. He wanted to hunt them for sport. They bred quickly, spread and became pests. A contagious disease called myxomatosis was introduced in 1950. It spread rapidly and greatly reduced rabbit numbers. Unfortunately the rabbits have built up an immunity to the disease and scientists are looking for a replacement that is effective.

 A cactus known as prickly pear was an introduced cactus species that spread to become a great pest in Australia. In 1926 a moth called cactoblastis that fed on prickly pear was introduced and the pest plant was controlled after just a few years.

 Blow flies use cattle dung pats to lay their eggs. These flies also lay their eggs directly onto sheep causing what is known as blowfly strike as the maggots feed on the living sheep. Most affected sheep die painful deaths.

Dung beetles were introduced into Australia in the 1970s to control fly numbers. Like blowflies, these beetles lay their eggs in dung. They then roll the dung into a ball and bury it. This reduces the number of sites in which flies can lay their eggs. In 1990 assassin bugs from Queensland were released in citrus orchards in NSW and Victoria to control citrus bugs (stink bugs). The patient work of scientists has helped us in the fight against species that are our competitors. They give meaning to the saying knowledge is power.

COMPREHENSION

1. Write short answers to these questions.

   a. Which creature became a pest after being introduced into Australia in 1935?
   _____

   b. Why did the cane toad's numbers grow to plague proportions?_____

   c. What did Thomas Austin release on his farm in 1859?_____

   d. What disease was used to control rabbit numbers? _____

   e. What does contagious mean?_____

   f. To which plant family does the prickly pear belong? _____

   g. Which moth was released to control the spread of prickly pear? _____

   h. Which animal is affected by blowfly strike? _____

   i. Which beetle was introduced to control fly numbers?_____

   j. Which bug is being used to protect citrus fruits from citrus bugs?_____

2. Write sentence answers to these questions.

   a. What is meant by the term biological control?_____
   _____

   b. Why were cane toads introduced into Australia? _____
   _____

   c. What is meant by blowfly strike?_____

   d. How does a dung beetle help reduce fly numbers? _____

3. Find words with these meanings in the text. First letters are given.

   a. work out d_____

   b. moves by water passing through substance l_____

   c. a collection of fruit trees o_____

   d. spoiled r_____

   e. killer a_____

   f. manure d_____

   g. fly grubs m_____

   h. makes less r_____

   i. set free r_____

Research: What is Paterson's Curse? Who call it Salvation Jane?

16. JAMES JOHNSON AND FREDERICK HEDGES SURVIVORS

Sydney Heads

On either side of the entrance to Sydney Harbour stand two imposing sandstone headlands. They are known simply as North Head and South Head or Sydney Heads. These headlands form a natural barrier to wild winds and waves, making Sydney Harbour one of the safest harbours in the world. Once inside them a ship is safe.

The Heads were, however, the site of one of Australia's worst shipping disasters.

The Dunbar was a clipper ship which left England, bound for Australia in 1857. On board were 59 crew and 63 passengers. The ship's captain, James Green, had made the journey numerous times before, without incident.

Having been pushed along by fair breezes he expected a safe docking on 20 August. As the ship came closer to Sydney Heads the wind began to blow fiercely. To make matters worse, torrential rain started to fall. This made visibility poor.

As he approached Sydney Heads Captain Green made an error that was to cost the lives of all but one person on the ship. Thinking he saw North Head through the murk and gloom the captain turned the ship to the west to begin entry to the harbour. He had, however, miscalculated. Dunbar had not yet cleared South Head. The wind and waves drove the ship onto the rocks of South Head. Only a young crewman, James Johnson, managed to cling to some debris from the broken ship. The waves washed him onto the rocks and he managed to clamber to safety — the sole survivor of the 122 that had set out from England.

Nine years later, on 12 July, 1866, James Johnson was to visit a similarly dreadful ordeal. Over a period of several days wild winds and storms lashed Australia's east coast. Twenty-four ships were lost in this time. One of these, a paddle wheeler called Cawarra, was washed onto some rocks at the entrance to Newcastle Harbour. These rocks, known as the Oyster Banks had taken ships before.

As the Cawarra was being pounded to matchwood James and two friends witnessed what was happening. He had been working at Newcastle Lighthouse. Narrowing his eyes he made out what appeared to be a sailor holding tightly to a buoy in the harbour's foaming waters.

James and his two friends managed to row a boat out to rescue the young seaman whose name was Frederick Hedges. Of the sixty people on board the Cawarra only Frederick survived.

It was a rare co-incidence. James, himself the sole survivor of a shipwreck, had rescued Frederick, another sole survivor.

COMPREHENSION

A. Write short answers below.

1. Which two headlands stand at the entrance to Sydney Harbour?_____

2. In which year was the Dunbar wrecked on the rocks of South Head? _____

3. Who was the only survivor of the wreck of the Dunbar?_____

4. How many people lost their lives when the Dunbar was wrecked?

_____

5. How many ships were wrecked in the storms that lashed the NSW coast in July 1866?

_____

6. Where was the Cawarra wrecked?_____

7. What were the rocks at the entrance to Newcastle Harbour called?

_____

8. How did Frederick Hedges keep afloat?_____

9. How many people died when the Cawarra was wrecked? _____

10. What unusual co-incidence occurred when James rescued Frederick?

_____

B. Find words with these meanings in the text. Some letters are given.

1. The place where something happened __ __ t __

2. the degree to which things can be seen __ __ s __ b __ __ __ __ __

3. mistake __ r __ __ __

4. rubbish or ruins   __ __ b __ __ __

5. the unlikely accidental occurrence of two or more events __ o __ __ __ __ d __ __ c __

C. Number the events in the order in which they took place. (Write 1 for first, 2 for second etc.)

1. There was nothing unusual about the weather when the Dunbar approached Sydney Heads in August 1857. _____

2. The rescue of one sole survivor of a shipwreck by another was one of the strangest stories in the annals of maritime history. _____

3. Because he could not see properly Captain Green drove Dunbar onto the rocks of South Head. _____

4. Two headlands are at the entrance to Sydney Harbour. _____

5. James Johnson rescued Frederick Hedges from a shipwreck. _____

6. The weather changed as Dunbar came near Sydney Heads. _____

7. In 1866 a ship called Cawarra entered Newcastle Harbour. _____

INDICATORS & OUTCOMES	**a.** answers literal (2, 3, 3, 5, 6, 7, 8 and 10) and literal (4 and 9) questions.
	b. uses context to work out the meaning of words
	c. can sequence events logically in a text

17. ALBERT NAMATJIRA

Albert Namatjira was an Arunta aborigine who was born in 1902. He grew up on the Hermannsburg Mission near Alice Spring's in the Northern Territory. The Mission was run by the Lutheran Church. As was often the case on such settlements, the difference between the beliefs of the tribal people and the people running the missions caused many misunderstandings. Because the Christian teachings were so different from their own, the tribal people often grew up filled with uncertainty.

Up to the age of thirteen Albert was educated by Christian missionaries. At that age he was initiated into manhood according to the customs of his tribe. So, two different streams of thought were part of his upbringing. Throughout his adult life it seemed that these influences caused him to be at odds with one

group or another. His marriage at the age of 18 to his sweetheart, Illkalita, wasn't approved by the tribal elders or the missionaries. The couple ran away and after three years returned to acceptance.

It was during a period of drought that people began to realise that Albert had artistic talent that was well above the ordinary. Money to run the mission came, in part, from the raising and sale of cattle. During the drought this became unprofitable. Pastor Albrecht, the man in charge, suggested that money could be made by manufacturing souvenirs. These were usually made of mulga wood. The wood was decorated with Aboriginal designs burnt into it with hot wire.

In 1934 the artist, Rex Batttarbee, visited the mission. He gave Albert some lessons in the use of watercolours. He saw that Albert had great talent and that he learnt quickly. Returning a year later, Battarbee gave Albert more lessons. Albert's landscape painting style was unique. He captured the country in which he lived like no-one before had done.

A series of successful exhibitions followed. These earned Albert enough money to build a house on the mission and to buy a truck which he used to carry his equipment when he went on painting trips into the outback. As he became increasingly successful, however, he came up against obstacles. It seemed that these had been put into place to remind him that Aborigines weren't supposed to rise above certain limits.

In 1949 he wanted to buy a cattle station but was denied a grazier's licence by authorities. A local law forbade Aborigines from being in the city of Adelaide after dark. When Albert wanted to buy some land to build a house there, this law denied him that right. According to the law of his tribe most of Albert's money went to supporting its more than 500 members. He was pursued by the Tax Office but most of his money had been distributed amongst his people. These three cases show how selectively the laws of that time discriminated against Aborigines. He had to pay taxes like a white Australian without recognition that the law of his people said that it must be shared amongst them. He was denied the right to run a business or choose where he lived. As well, all Aborigines at that time did not have the right to vote.

In 1957 he officially became a citizen of Australia. This entitled him to buy alcohol. When, in 1958, he did so he was arrested and charged with supplying alcohol to

Aborigines who were not regarded as citizens. In poor health and saddened by his treatment he died in 1959, a few months after his release from prison. His paintings remain to remind us not only of his great talent, but of a shameful chapter in our history.

ACTIVITY

A. FACT OR OPINION?

A FACT is something that is indisputably true. An OPINION is a judgement formed about something not necessarily based on fact or knowledge.

Write FACT or OPINION after each statement.

1. Albert grew up on Hermmansburg Mission. _____

2. Albert shouldn't have taken part in the initiation ceremony. _____

3. Rex Battarbee was a better painter than William Dobell. _____

4. Albert used his money to help the people of his tribe. _____

5. If Albert's money hadn't been used to buy alcohol he would not have gone to gaol.

   _____

B. Rule lines to match each CAUSE with its EFFECT.

CAUSE	EFFECT
1. Cattle raising became unprofitable.	The Taxation Department pursued Albert.
2. Rex Battarbee visited Hermannsburg.	Albert was unable to build a house in Adelaide.
3. Elders and missionaries disapproved of his marriage	Aborigines began making souvenirs to sell.
4. Albert's paintings made him some money.	Albert and Ilkalita ran away.
5. A law did not allow Aborigines into Adelaide after dark.	Albert got some training in the use of watercolours.

C. Imagine you are going to interview Albert. Write a question you would ask him. Pool questions to make up a question bank.

D. Choose the correct words from the word bank to fill the gaps.

Lutheran	discriminatory	tribal	Battarbee	souvenirs
		exhibitions		

1. Albert grew up on a mission run by the _____ Church.

2. He learnt Christian and _____ teachings.

3. The first signs of his artistic talent showed when the mission turned to making _____

   _____.

4. The artist Rex _____ gave Albert some lessons in the use of watercolours.

5. Albert began to make money from his paintings after a number of _____ _____.

6. He was unable to do a number of things due to _____ laws.

ACTIVITY

ALBERT NAMATJIRA   ENRICHMENT ACTIVITY

E. Write 'FACT' or 'OPINION' after each statement.

    a. Albert grew up on Hermmansburg Mission._____

    b. Albert shouldn't have taken part in the initiation ceremony._____

    c. Rex Battarbee was a better painter than William Dobell._____

    d. Albert used his money to help the people of his tribe._____

    e. If Albert's money hadn't been used to buy alcohol, he wouldn't have gone to gaol._____

F. Rule lines to match each cause with an effect.

CAUSE	EFFECT
a. Cattle raising became unprofitable.	The Taxation Department pursued him.
b. Rex Battarbee visited Hermannsburg.	Albert was unable to build a house in
c. Elders and missionaries disapproved of his marriage.	Aborigines began making souvenirs to sell.
d. Albert's paintings made him some money.	Albert and Ilkalita ran away.
e. A law said that Aborigines were not allowed into Adelaide agter dark.	Albert got some training in the use of watercolours.

G. Imagine you are going to interview Albert Namatjira. Write one question you would like to ask him. Pool questions to make up a question bank.

_____

_____

H. Choose the correct words from the word bank to fill the gaps.

discriminatory Lutheran tribal Battarbee souvenirs exhibitions

a. Albert grew up on a mission run by the _____Church.

b. He learnt Christian and _____ teachings.

c. The first signs of his artistic talent showed when the mission turned to making _____.

d. The artist Rex _____ gave Albert some lessons using watercolours.

e. Albert began to make money from his paintings after a number of _____.

f. He was unable to do a number of things that he wanted because of _____ laws.

I. Notemaking is an important skill. In general, when making notes you use only the important nouns (naming words), verbs (doing words) and adjectives (describing words) to make your notes. These words are bold in the sentences above.
Write the bold words in point form to make notes about Albert Namatjira below. The first point has been written for you.

  - grew up on mission run by Church _____

_____

_____

_____

Notice in the picture above how the road appears to become narrower and the telegraph poles smaller? The artist has used an artistic device called PERSPECTIVE to give the impression of depth. In reality the road does not get narrower, nor the poles smaller. The artist is tricking our eyes making a 2D flat picture appear to have 3D depth. The point at which the sides of the road come together is known as the VANISHING POINT.

Draw your own perspective picture below. To become a good artist requires natural skill but, also, a good deal of learning of artist techniques.

18. PHAR LAP

The 1930s was the era of the Great Depression around the world. A depression is a period when there is little economic activity. Many companies close down and people lose their jobs. Just as in other countries, times in Australia were hard. Despite the economic difficulties, sport-loving Australians saw this period as a golden era. Four champions, recognised as perhaps the greatest of all time in their fields graced the scene. They were Hubert Opperman – a cyclist, Don Bradman – a cricketer, Walter Lindrum – a billiards and snooker champion and a racehorse, Phar Lap.

Phar Lap (it means lightning in the Thai language) came to Australia from New Zealand early in 1927. His trainer, Harry Telford, convinced wealthy American, David J Davis, to buy the horse. Although he wasn't really interested, Telford's constant urging eventually won the day and Davis bought the big chestnut for $330, a small amount to pay for a racehorse, even in those times.

Around the stable, Phar Lap was called Bobby. Young stable hand, Tommy Woodcock, looked after Bobby. He became Bobby's great friend. The horse would not eat unless Tommy was there. Phar Lap's first few races gave no clue that he was a racehorse that would soon be regarded by many people as the greatest of all time. When he won his first race he began a pattern that would soon become familiar. Newcastle jockey, Jim Pike, was his regular rider.

The Melbourne Cup is Australia's greatest horse race. For about 3 minutes and 20 seconds on the first Tuesday of each November the country stops to either watch or listen to a broadcast of this great sporting event. Large amounts of money are gambled on the race. Some bookmakers (people who take bets (wagers) on horse races) stood to lose a lot of money if Phar Lap won the race in 1930. Telford received anonymous phone calls telling him to scratch (withdraw) the horse from the race or risk it being harmed. The police were informed and Tommy Woodcock stayed with the horse at all times, even sleeping in the stables.

On race morning, as Tommy was leading Phar Lap to Flemington Racecourse, a large car drove past, blowing its horn. A shotgun was fired out of the window but Tommy swung the horse around and both were unharmed. Phar Lap went on to win the race easily. It was decided that Phar Lap was now ready to take on the world.

In 1932, after a sea journey of 16 000 kilometres, he arrived in the USA to run in the highest prize-money race ($140 000) ever held at that time. It was at a racecourse called Agua Caliente in Mexico. Phar Lap won the 2 000 metre race easily, defeating the best horses in the world. But 16 days later the great horse was dead. The dew-covered alfalfa he had eaten early one morning caused a build-up of gas in his stomach. It was this that killed him.

So popular was this mighty horse that, even in death, he remains a great attraction. His body was preserved by some taxidermists and is still on display in Museum Victoria.

Tommy Woodcock went on to become a successful and much-loved trainer of racehorses.

In an interview before the running of the 1965 Melbourne Cup, jockey Jim Pike said, '...people may think I would like to be there, but I don't mind missing it. I rode the greatest horse of all and everything's been an anti-climax ever since.'

COMPREHENSION

A. Write short answers below.

1. What did many companies do during the Great Depression of the 1930? _____

2. What was the result of this for many people? _____

3. With which sport was Hubert Opperman associated? _____

4. With which sport was Don Bradman associated? _____

5. With which sport was Walter Lindrum associated? _____

6. What does the name Phar Lap mean? _____

7. From which country's language does the name Phar Lap come? _____

8. Who was Phar Lap's trainer?_____

9. In which country was Phar Lap foaled (born) ?_____

10. What was Phar Lap's stable name? _____

11. Who was the stable hand who looked after Phar Lap? _____

12. Who rode Phar Lap in most of his wins? _____

13. On which day of which month is the Melbourne Cup run? _____

14. In which year did Phar Lap win this great race? _____

15. What caused Phar Lap's death? _____

16. Where can you see Phar Lap today? _____

B. Jim Pike said that after his association with Phar Lap everything that followed had ben an anticlimax. Write the dictionary definition of climax.

_____

Now write the dictionary definition of anticlimax.

_____

C. What is meant by a horse's sire and dam? Use a dictionary to find the answers.

1. _____

2. Who was Phar Lap's sire? _____

3. Who was his dam? _____

INDICATORS & **OUTCOMES**	**a.** answers literal questions
	b. (B) & (C) can use an online dictionary to find word meanings

Cricket is a game with a rich and interesting history. Don Bradman's ability was such that he remains a household name in countries where the game is played even though he played his last game more than half a century ago.

Many followers of sports enjoy discussions about which player was the 'greatest'. Usually there are several contenders. This isn't the case in cricket. Few people would argue that Bradman was not the greatest player of all time.

Cricket is a game in which a person's talent can be measured quite well using statistics (numbers). Bradman's statistics make him almost twice as good as the next best player in the history of the game.

Don Bradman was born in Cootamundra, NSW in 1908. Most of his growing up was done in the pretty NSW Southern Highlands town of Bowral. As a boy he loved bat and ball games. He invented games that he could play by himself. One of these involved throwing a golf ball against a water tank and hitting it with a narrow cricket stump when it rebounded. Constantly playing these games as a child, young Don was developing his reflexes and ball sense.

He was chosen to tour England with the Australian test match team in 1930. On this tour he averaged an amazing 139 runs for each test match innings.

Because of his ability to win matches single-handedly, the English team that toured Australia for the 1932 -33 season used an unsporting tactic called 'bodyline' to try to counteract his great talent. This involved bowling the ball at the batsman's body (often the head) and placing all the players on one side of the wicket. This is considered one of the greatest sporting controversies of the 20th century. It even threatened to lead to poor relations between England and Australia at a government level. The tactic was quickly made illegal by cricket's world governing body.

In his career Don Bradman averaged 99.94 runs per test match innings. If he had scored four runs in his last test innings instead of a 'duck'(zero) his average would have been exactly 100.

Importantly, however, despite his individual talent, he realised that he was playing a team sport and representing his country. In an interview he said, 'Anybody has to be proud to represent their country, whether it be cricket or football, or whatever it may be. It is vastly more important to represent your country than it is to represent yourself.'

If you go to Bowral you may visit a museum that shows things from Australia's cricketing history. It is called the Bradman Museum. Nearby is Bradman Oval where young Don played his early cricket.

DON BRADMAN COMPREHENSION CROSSWORD

Highest Test
Score: 334

Highest First
Class Score: 452

Tests: 52

Runs: 6996

Average: 99.94

Across

1. A score in cricket is called a '_____'.
3. When you bowl six balls it is called an '_____' in cricket.
7. Opposite of 'out'.
8. Curriculum Vitae (initials)
9. Don Bradman grew up in this town.
10. Articles of clothing.
11. What a bowler does in cricket.
12. If you get out in a game of cricket without scoring any runs you are said to have made a '_____'.
13. You hit the ball with one of these.
14. A chicken.
16. At Bowral there is one of these dedicated to Don Bradman.
19. The number of players on a cricket team.
22. Rugs.
23. Ante Meridian (initials).
25. The unsporting tactic used by the English team of 1932-33.
27. As a boy. Don Bradman hit one of these balls aginst a water tank.
30. Wrist is to hand as '_____' is to foot.
31. Bowral is a country '_____'
33. What Don hit the golf ball with when it rebounded from the water tank.
37. Mount '_____' is a town in Western Queensland.
38. Don Bradman was born in this NSW town.

Down

1. Tear.
2. United Nations (initials).
3. The ground on which young Don Bradman played is now called Bradman '_____'.
4. Not difficult.
5. Opposite of 'stop'.
6. The game that Don Bradman played.
8. It gives us milk.
9. Bachelor of Arts (initials).
10. A baby's bed.
11. The thing you hit in cricket.
12. A tom-tom is one.
14. Him
15. Don toured this country with the Australian cricket team in 1930.
17. Past tense of 'sing'.
18. You and I
20. You can record something from television using this kind of tape.
21. Don threw a golf ball against a water '_____'.
24. Short form if the names 'Melvin' and 'Melanie'.
26. Not out.
28. If you hit the ball to the fence in cricket you score this number of runs.
29. 'Not Out' (initials).
31. A group of three is called this.
32. Opposite of 'downs'.
33. The Earth goes around this star.
34. Murrumbidgee Irrigation Area (initials).
35. Before Christ (initials).
36. Western Australia (initials).

You will need:

three dice (2 for the bowler and one for the batting team) a pen or pencil and paper to keep score

Rules:

* Roll a die to see who bats or bowls. The person rolling the higher number bats first.

* The bowler rolls first using 2 dice. If a double (two of the same number) is bowled the person batting is out. If a double isn't rolled, the person playing for the batting team rolls and scores the number rolled. This is written on the score sheet 'runs' column.

* When the ten players written on the batting side are out, the players swap places.

* The team with the highest total wins.

EXAMPLE:

BLOGGS   4 3 6 1 2 5 1 1 3 >

26   The first 9 balls bowled by the bowler did not result in doubles. The person playing for the batting team rolled 4 after the first 'bowl', 3 after the second and so on. The 10th ball bowled was a 'double 'so Bloggs was declared 'out'. (>) Have fun choosing your team. You can include friends, real cricketers, relatives etc.

TEAM 1

Team Name

Batter

Runs   **Score**

Runs	Score
/	/
/	/
/	/
/	/
/	/
/	/
/	/
/	/
/	/
/	/
	TOTAL /

TEAM 2

Team Name

Batter

Runs		Score
/		/
/		/
/		/
/		/
/		/
/		/
/		/
/		/
/		/
/		/
	TOTAL	/

20. JOHN SIMPSON (KIRKPATRICK)

When World War broke out in 1914 John Simpson was quick to enlist in the AIF (Australian Imperial Forces). Simpson was an Englishman whose real name was John Simpson Kirkpatrick. Because he had deserted ship while serving in the British Merchant Navy in 1910, he did not use his real name when he enlisted.

He was given the job of stretcher bearer and was part of the ANZAC (Australian And New Zealand Army Corps) landing at Gallipoli on 25 April, 1915.

The life of the field ambulance man was dangerous. These men were generally not armed and had to try to avoid being shot while carrying the wounded on stretchers so they could receive medical attention behind the lines.

Donkeys had been brought to Gallipoli by the ANZACS to carry water. Simpson realised that he could carry wounded men to safety using these animals. Usually it took two men to carry one wounded soldier. With his donkey (called 'Murphy' in some accounts and Ábdul' or 'Duffy'in others), he worked tirelessly and saved many lives. To the soldiers on the battlefield it seemed as if he was protected by a guardian angel. Time after time he faced heavy gunfire, only to return unscathed with a wounded man. On 9 May, 1915, however his ángel' deserted him. He was killed by shrapnel from an exploding shell.

His selfless disregard for personal safety typified the ANZAC spirit. There is a memorial to Simpson and his donkey in the form of a bronze sculpture near Melbourne's Shrine of Remembrance. The mascot of the 1st Field Hospital is a donkey named Private Simpson. It took part in the unit's anniversary parade in 1998.

Read the ACROSTIC poem then write your own on the lines:

Soldier lying over in 'No Man's Land'.
If we are quick and careful we could get him back here.
Murphy, faithful friend, there's work to be done.
Pull him up, I will. He's wounded but he'll live.
Steady there, Murphy. It's nearly time.
Out of here now! Let's go!
Now then, Murphy, didn't I tell you not to worry?

....

S_____

I_____

M_____

P_____

S_____

O_____

N_____

Across

1. Courageous
3. Simpson used a donkey to _____ wounded soldiers.
4. A period of time.
5. Murphy was one of these.
8. Arafura Sea (initials).
10. Opposite of 'yes'.
12. The name given to an Australian or New Zealand soldier who fought at Gallipoli.
13. A glow worm does this.
15. You sleep in one.
17. The place where the ANZACs landed.
19. Abbreviation for 'sergeant'
21. Male equivalent of 'Ma'.
22. Short form of the name Alan
24. Opposite of stop.
25. Abbreviation for 'road'
26. Not cooked.
28. Many soldiers '_____ at Gallipoli.
30. One of the names of Simpson's donkey.
32. The surname under which John Simpson Kirkpatrick enlisted in the army.
35. Fire produces this.
36. One of the names of Simpson's donkey.

Down

1. The sculpture of Simpson is made out of this.
2. Royal Australian Navy (initials).
4. Short for Edward.
6. You do this to a soccer ball.
7. Opposite of no.
8. It was as if an _____ were watching over Simpson.
9. An Anzac was one of these.
11. The fourth month of the year.
12. Australian Imperial Forces (initials).
14. Sheep produce this.
15. A bayonet has a sharp _____.
16. What a chicken lays.
18. The month in which ANZAC day falls.
20. Simpson went '__' and fro picking up the wounded
22. Soldiers make up the '____'
23. Los Angeles (initials).
27. Donkeys were brought to Gallipoli to carry this.
28. One of the names of Simpson's donkey.
29. Abbreviation for 'captain'.
31. Simpsons first name.
32. Female form of 'he'.
33. The abbreviation that means 'that is' (id est).
34. The month in which Simpson was killed.

PROPAGANDA is one-sided information of a political nature that is spread to influence people's opinions. The posters below are examples of propaganda used during World War I.

1.   How is the first poster trying to influence men to enlist in the army?

_____

_____

_____

2.   The 'mad brute' in the second poster is meant to be a German (Hun) soldier. How is it meant to influence people to enlist?

_____

_____

_____

3.   STEREOTYPING is a favoureed technique of the propagandist. Write the dictionary meaning of STEREOTYPE.

_____

_____

_____

4.   Another favoured method of the propagandist is DEHUMANISATION. Write the dictionary meaning of DEHUMANISE.

_____

_____

Draw and colour your own propaganda poster here.

21. SIR DOUGLAS MAWSON

Douglas Mawson was born in England but his parents came to Australia when he was just a child. He was a good student and when he finished his studies became a lecturer in science (mineralogy) at the University of Adelaide.

At this time there was a great deal of interest in exploring the polar icecaps. Because of his background in science Mawson was, in 1908, asked to  join an expedition to find out more about Antarctica. The leader of this expedition was the famed English polar explorer, Ernest Shackleton. This type of exploration was very dangerous. Exposure to the extreme cold could very quickly kill a person.

On this expedition Mawson and his fellow explorers climbed Mount Erebus, Antarctica's second highest volcano (3 794 metres) after Mount Sidley (4 285 metres). Arriving at the mountain had meant a journey of over 2 000 kilometres and suffering from severe frostbite.

Mawson led a second expedition to Antarctica in 1911. Its main purpose was to study the Australian sector of Antarctica. When they arrived the party split up into 5 groups. Each was to explore a different region and then return to the base camp. Mawson was in a group of three with the Englishman, Belgrave Ninnis, and Xavier Metz, a champion skier from Switzerland. This was to be a tragic journey.

It soon became clear that they had miscalculated the amount of food they would need to complete their mission. Because of the tremendous physical demands of travel over the snow and ice their bodies burnt far more fuel than they normally would have. Their food ran low and rations had to be reduced to a tiny amount for each man. They ate biscuits and seal meat and used the same tea leaves over and over again.

The area was crossed by deep cracks in the ice called crevasses. They were often concealed by a covering of soft snow called a 'snow bridge'. Anyone unfortunate enough to break through such a snow bridge and falling down a crevasse would almost certainly not survive.

 When they were 500 kilometres from their base camp, Ninnis disappeared down a crevasse. With him went their tent and most of their remaining food. Mawson and Metz turned back. They would crawl under a piece of canvas to shelter when they rested. When their food ran out, they ate the dogs. Nothing was wasted. Even the paws were stewed and eaten. Within three weeks Mertz died of starvation.

Mawson struggled on alone for twenty days. When his soles began to separate from his feet he tied them on. He crawled a large part of the way on all fours. As he finally struggled in to his base camp he saw his ship, the Aurora, well out to sea and moving away.

Some men, however, had set up a camp and stayed behind in case the party returned. They nursed Mawson, the sole survivor of the trio, back to health. On returning to Australia in 1914 he was knighted and received many awards of recognition.

Despite his terrible ordeal, Mawson set out again to explore the Antarctic coastline by ship in 1929 and 1931. The main Australian base in Antarctica is named after this brave man.

COMPREHENSION

SIR DOUGLAS MAWSON   COMPREHENSION / CLOSE

Read the story of Douglas Mawson and find the correct words from the word bank to fill the gaps. There are five words that do not belong.

Switzerland	stayed	parents	wife	Ninnis	Bagshot	Aurora
crevasse	Antarctica	Magnetic	pulled	twenty	mineralogy	
penguins	David	Adelaide	five	sled	expedition	
starvation	Egypt	poodles	separated	food	on	

Mawson came to Australia with his __ __ __ __ __ t __ when he was a child. He became a lecturer in __ __ n __ __ __ __ __ __ __ __ at the University of __ __ __ __ __ __ d __ . His first major mission was when he accompanied Edgeworth __ __ v __ __ to explore __ __ t __ __ __ __ __ __ __ . This expedition was the first to reach the __ __ g __ __ __ __ __ South Pole.

Mawson led a second __ x __ __ __ __ t __ __ __ to Antarctica in 1911.

When his party arrived they broke up into __ __ v __ different groups.

In Mawson's group was an Englishman called Belgrave __ __ n __ __ __ and Xavier Mertz, a skiing champion from __ __ __ __ z __ __ __ __ __ __ .

When they were five hundred kilometres from the base camp Ninnis disappeared down a deep __ __ __ __ __ __ s __ __ . Mertz and Mawson pressed on. When their __ __ o __ ran out they had to eat the __ __ e __ dogs. After three weeks Mertz died of __ __ __ __ __ v __ __ __ __ __ __ . Mawson struggled __ __ alone. His soles __ __ p __ __ __ t __ __ from his feet , but he bound them back on. He fell down a crevasse while pulling his sled . Luckily the sled became stuck . After dangling from the straps for some time he __ __ __ __ e __ himself out. He reached the base camp after __ w __ __ __ __ days only to see his ship, the __ __ r __ __ __ , disappearing over the horizon. Luckily, some men had __ __ __ y __ __ behind in the hope he would return

Australian History Comprehension Year 6
Gunter Schymkiw

83

© 2017 Five Senses Education Pty Ltd

22. FRED HOLLOWS

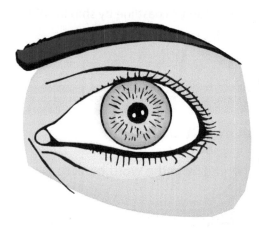

At a dinner one evening Fred Hollows found himself sitting near the Premier of New South Wales, Nick Greiner. When, during the course of a conversation, the politician said, 'Of course, self-motivation or self-gain is the basic motivation.'

'Professor Hollows disagreed with him. 'You're wrong,' he said. 'That's animal motivation. Human motivation is looking after the old, the lame and the blind; the people less fortunate than yourself.'

The things that he mentioned were certainly the forces that drove him. Born in New Zealand in 1929, Fred Hollows came to Australia in 1965.

As a young man he tried numerous jobs, and was considering a future as a clergyman before he settled on the study of Medicine.

In 1968 he went to Wattie Creek in the Northern Territory. He was one of a group of visiting doctors doing medical work among aboriginal stockmen there. What he found shocked him.

A large number of the men had the eye condition known as Labrador keratopathy. This condition affected their eyesight, eventually leading to blindness. It was caused by the men having too little protection from the sun's rays as they worked outside all day.

As he continued to work in the outback, Fred repeatedly saw people in similar circumstances. He worked hard to establish the National Trachoma And Eye Health Program in 1976. This program continues to provide eye care to people in over 400 remote outback communities. Professor Hollows and his team travelled the outback, performing over 30 000 operations for trachoma, and restoring the sight of affected people.

He was given numerous awards, but refused an Order Of Australia in 1985 for his work in aboriginal health. He felt that if he accepted such an award it would send the signal that aboriginal health was being adequately attended to. He felt that there was still far too much to be done for such an award to have any meaning.

Seeing a need for his work in other countries, Professor Hollows travelled to Vietnam, Burma, Thailand and Eritrea. Here he educated people in eye care and established facilities that would allow local doctors to carry on his work after he had left.

In 1989 Fred Hollows was diagnosed with cancer. Despite his worsening condition, he continued his work until his death in 1993. In accordance with his wishes, he was buried in Bourke, a town in the outback. He had always said that the outback was 'the real Australia.'

A. Write short answers below where appropriate (questions 2 to 20).

1. Write the dictionary definition of ***motivation.***

2. What did Fred Hollows say was human motivation? _____

3. When and where was Fred Hollows born? _____

4. When did he come to Australia? _____

5. What did he study at University? _____

6. In which Australian state or territory is Wattie Creek? _____

7. Who were Doctor Hollows' patients at Wattie Creek? _____

8. From which eye condition did many of the stockmen suffer? _____

9. What caused this ailment? _____

10. What did this condition usually lead to? _____

11. What did Doctor Hollows help to establish in 1976? _____

12. Approximately how many eye operations did Doctor Hollows and his team perform?
    _____

13. Which honour did Doctor Hollows refuse in 1985? _____

14. Why did he refuse this honour?_____

15. In which four countries did Doctor Hollows establish eye care clinics? _____
    _____

16. Which of these countries is in Africa? _____

17. With which illness was Doctor Hollows diagnosed in 1989? _____

18. In which year did Doctor Hollows die? _____

19. Where was he buried? _____

20. What part of Australia did Doctor Hollows say was the real Australia? _____
    _____

B. The title *doctor* is one that is hard-earned. There is so much to know in many branches of medicine that some doctors specialise in treating one particular part of the body. For example, a chiropodist specialises in treating the feet, a stomatologist, the mouth etc. Use a dictionary to match the medical specialists with the part of the body they treat.

oculist   dentist   gastrologist   cardiologist   audiologist
nephrologist   dermatologist   neurologist   osteologist   haematologist

1.   teeth = _____

2.   eyes = _____

3.   ears = _____

4.   stomach = _____

5.   kidney = _____

6.   bones = _____

7.   brain = _____

8.   heart = _____

9.   blood = _____

10.   skin = _____

ACTIVITY

A. The story, 'The Country Of The Blind 'was written by the famous author, HG Wells. It tells of the life of some people in an isolated valley in South America's Andes Mountains. Here is a brief outline.

Hundreds of years ago an illness had infected all of the people who lived in a remote, isolated valley in the AndesMountains. It made all of the people living there blind. The blindness also afflicted later generations so that any person born there was also without sight. The people came to have no knowledge at all of sight.

When a visitor accidently stumbles upon their valley he is amazed by the way in which the inhabitants have adjusted to being unsighted.

Many of the things they did, while not sensible for sighted people, were very sensible for people without sight.

For example, they worked at night when it was cool and slept during the heat of day.

The stranger begins to adjust to living with these people and, in the end, must make a difficult choice.

Write two ways that your life would change if you suddenly lost the power of sight. What things that you currently enjoy doing would you be unable to do? What might be some new interests?

_____

_____

_____

_____

B. In HG Wells' story Nunez, the stranger who stumbles upon the country of the blind, thinks of the proverb 'In the country of the blind the one eyed man is king.' Explain this proverb's meaning.

_____

_____

_____

_____

C. Do this exercise with a partner under a teacher's supervision. Take turns to ensure that neither of you puts yourself in danger. Close your eyes and try moving around your classroom or an area in your school's playground. What do you notice? How does your walk change? Does this exercise help you to understand why animals with poor or no eyesight often have very long antennae? Write comments below.

_____

_____

_____

_____

INDICATORS & OUTCOMES	**a.** responds to themes and issues raised by a text
	b. identifies symbolic meaning
	c. considers events in a text from a personal point of view

For a country with such a small population, Australia has a proud record in the arts (music, theatre, painting, sculpture and writing). Four women who won respect for Australia on the world's stages were the singers Dame Nellie Melba, Gladys Moncrieff, June Bronhill and Dame Joan Sutherland.

Nellie Melba (1861–1931) was born Helen Porter Mitchell in Melbourne . She called herself Melba after her home city. In 1887 Melba went to Europe to perform in some of the great opera houses. Fifteen years later, and by now world famous, she returned to tour Australia. Melba's career lasted until 1928. Two dishes, Peach Melba and Melba Toast were named after her. Nellie gave many 'farewell 'concerts around the world. From this came the saying to do a Melba. This means to announce one's departure, but then make numerous comebacks. Nellie was a great pioneer. She set an example for the talented singers who followed her. Australian artists realised that they could be the equal of any in the world.

Gladys Moncrieff (1892–1976) began her singing career in Townsville, Queensland. For over 35 years Our Glad, as she was known, entertained audiences in Australia, New Zealand, England and South Africa. She appeared in war zones to entertain the troops who were serving during World War II and the Korean War.

June Gough (1929–2005) was born in Broken Hill, New South Wales. After appearing in a number of competitions, the people of Broken Hill began to realise that they had a great talent in their midst. They raised enough money to allow her to go to England to study. In gratitude she changed her surname to Bronhill, after the city. June went on to have an illustrious career as a singer and stage actor.

Dame Joan Sutherland's (1926–2010) career spanned over 40 years. She was recognised as one ot the 20th century's finest voices. In Italy they called her La Stupenda, which means The Wonderful One. She made more complete operatic recordings than any other singer in history. She frequently returned to Australia to give performances.

The music of great composers and performing artists enriches our lives.

ACTIVITY

A. Write short answers to the questions below.

1. What was Nellie Melba's real name? _____

2. Why did she choose *Melba* as a stage name? _____

3. Where did she go to perform?_____

4. Which two dishes were named after her?

_____ and _____

5. What does 'to do a Melba 'mean? _____

6. What did Australian performers begin to realise as a result of the example set Melba? _____

7. Where did Gladys Moncrieff's singing career begin? _____

8. By what name was Gladys affectionately known? _____

9. What was June Bronhill's real name? _____

10. After which city did she take on her stage name? _____

11. What nickname was Joan Sutherland given? _____

12. What does this nickname mean? _____

B. Match the words to the songs. Write the song titles beside their words. (Hint: Type the words into a computer search engine.)

The Drover's Dream	**On The Road To Gundagai**	**Waltzing Matilda**
Our Don Bradman	**I've Been Everywhere**	**Advance Australia Fair**

1. 'There's a track winding back…" _____

2. 'Who is it that all Australia raves about… _____

3. 'Beneath our radiant Southern Cross… ' _____

4. 'Under the shade of a coolabah tree…' _____

5. 'One day while travelling sheep, my companions lay asleep… ' _____

6. 'Crossed the deserts fair, Man…' _____

C. A STATEMENT is a sentence that tells us something.

A QUESTION is a sentence that asks something. The sentence below is mixed up. Use all the words to write a STATEMENT, then a QUESTION.

June	born	was	Broken	Gough	Hill	in

STATEMENT: _____

QUESTION: _____

D. SKIMMING Locate these words in the text then write them in the order in which they appear on the information page.

enriches	farewell	example	population	gratitude	serving	pioneer

_____

_____

 **ACTIVITY**

Use the internet to find the answers below. Circle and highlight the answer you find to be correct. Don't guess.

1. Transported to Australia for horse-stealing at the age of 13, she became Australia's first highly successful business woman. Her name was…
    a. Mary Reiby
    b. Caroline Chisholm
    c. Margaret Holmes-A'Court
    d. Lady Mary Splatt

2. Leaving Sydney Harbour in her yacht, ***First Lady***, on 29th November 1989 and returning on June 5th 1988, this woman was the first to sail solo and non-stop around the world.
    a. Frances Drake
    b. Kylie Minogue
    c. Kay Cottee
    d. the 'Unsinkable' Molly Brown

3. She became the first woman aviatrix to fly from Australia to England in 1933. Despite many setbacks, including a near collision with a buffalo on a landing field, she succeeded. She spent 160 hours in the air doing this. She was….
    a. Maude Rose (Lores) Bonney
    b. Amelia Earhart
    c. Amy Johnson
    d. Mavis Baggs

4. This woman was a spy who worked with the French Resistance against the Nazis during World War II.
    a. Agent K-13
    b. Mata Hari
    c. Nancy Wake
    d. Edith Piaf

5. This woman wrote the best known poem about Australia, 'My Country'.
    a. Dorothy Wall
    b. Dorothea MacKellar
    c. May Gibbs
    d. Pamela Lyndon (P L) Travers

6. This brave nurse survived being machine-gunned by Japanese soldiers in a massacre during World War II. She hid her wounds when recaptured and spent more than three years as a prisoner-of-war. She gave evidence about the massacre at a War Crimes trial.
   a. Sister Kenny
   b. Germaine Greer
   c. Ita Buttrose
   d. Vivian Bullwinkle

7. The best-selling author of such books as *The Thornbirds*, Tim and *The First Man In Rome* is….
   a. Colleen McCullough
   b. Amelia Cuenca
   c. Judith Wright
   d. Miles Franklin

8. As well as being Queensland's first Aboriginal teacher, this woman studied law and became Australia's first Aboriginal barrister.
   a. Lowitja O'Donoghue
   b. Shirley 'Mum Shirl' Smith
   c. Patricia O'Shane
   d. Linda Burney

9. The first woman elected to Parliament. She had 12 children (6 sons and 6 daughters). She was…..
   a. Pauline Hansen
   b. Dame Enid Lyons
   c. Edna Everage
   d. Nicole Kidman

10. This champion swimmer became known as 'Australia's Mermaid'. In 1910 in Boston, USA, she was arrested and charged with indecent exposure for wearing a one piece bathing suit. The design soon became popular because it was comfortable and practical.
    a. Dawn Fraser
    b. Shane Gould
    c. Dame Edna Everage
    d. Annette Kellerman

11. This 16 year old girl helped rescue people from a shipwreck by riding her horse into the surf and dragging them to safety.
   a. Grace Darling
   b. Sister Mary MacKillop
   c. Grace Bussell
   d. Samantha Stosur

12. This woman is one of the world's most successful models. She was known around the world as 'The Body'.
   a. Margaret Court
   b. Eva Cox
   c. Jennifer Hawkins
   d. Elle MacPherson

13. This woman, born without the use of her legs, became a champion wheelchair athlete.
   a. Louise Sauvage
   b. Jana Pitman
   c. Ruth Park
   d. Joan Sutherland

14. This author and illustrator is best known for her characters 'Snugglepot 'and 'Cuddlepie'.
   a. Elizabeth Harrower
   b. Henry Handel Richardson
   c. May Gibbs
   d. Elisa Frazer

15. This aboriginal woman was the champion Australian runner of the 1990s. She won the gold medal for the 800m race at the 2 000 Olympics.
   a. Cathy Freeman
   b. Kath Walker
   c. Melinda Gainsford
   d. Betty Cuthbert

16. In 1987 this woman became the first female jockey to ride a horse in the Melbourne Cup.
   a. Maree Lyndon
   b. Beverly Buckingham
   c. Maureen Dittman
   d. Terese Payne

17. Elected to W A's State Parliament in 1921, she was the first woman to win a seat in any Australian parliament.
   a. Mary Bryant
   b. Edith Cowan
   c. Sarah Redfern
   d. Bronwyn Bishop

18. Australia's first woman Prime Minister…..
    a. Julia Gillard
    b. Dame Zara Bates
    c. Julie Bishop
    d. Joan Kirner

19. This woman didn't really exist but her 'show 'in the 1960s was a landmark in Australian television comedy.
    a. Mavis Bramston
    b. Cheryl Kernot
    c. Phyllis Diller
    d. Betty Blokkbuster

20. Herslf a distinguished English dancer, this woman went on to create and become artistic director of the Australian Ballet from 1962 to 1974.
    a. Gwen Plumb
    b. Kate Ceberano
    c. Dame Peggy Van Praagh
    d. Helen Reddy

 **ACTIVITY**

Use the internet to find the answers below. Circle and highlight the answer you find to be correct. Don't guess.

1. Australia's first Prime Minister was…
    a. George Washington
    b. Edmund Barton
    c. Alfred Deakin
    d. John Howard

2. The first Europeans to find a way across the Blue Mountains and open up the rich farmland to the west were…..
    a. Hunter, King and Bligh
    b. Blaxland, Lawson and Wentworth
    c. Kennedy and Galmahra
    d. Scott, Oates and Bowers

3. These brave but inexperienced explorers perished in the desert in their attempt to be the first to cross Australia from south to north.
   a. Burke and Wills
   b. Hume and Hovell
   c. Eyre and Wylie
   d. Bass and Flinders

4. The stress of being Australia's Prime Minister during World War II led to this man's sudden death not long after the war ended. He was a relatively young 60.
   a. Joseph Lyons
   b. Harold Holt
   c. Sir Robert Menzies
   d. John Curtin

5. After winning the Victoria Cross for bravery during World War II and later losing a leg through machine gun fire, this great man became Governor of NSW from 1966 to 1981.....
   a. Sir Isaac Isaacs
   b. Sir Roden Cutler
   c. Sir John Kerr
   d. Sir Henry Bolte

6. This man's real name was Arthur Hoey Davis. He wrote stories about farming in Australia and created the characters Dad and Dave.
   a. Banjo Paterson
   b. Sir Les Paterson
   c. Steele Rudd
   d. Morris West

7. Born in Denmark, this architect designed the modern marvel; Sydney's Opera House.
   a. Joern Utzon
   b. Walter Burley Griffin
   c. Frank Lloyd Wright
   d. Christopher Wren

8. This scientist and medical researcher made important discoveries which led to advances in the treatment of influenza and polio. He won a Nobel Prize for his study of the human immune system.
   a. Sir MacFarlane Burnet
   b. Sir Mark Oliphant
   c. Julius Sumner Miller
   d. Harry Messel

9. This man worked tirelessly in dreadful conditions to complete the Overland Telegraph Line. This linked Adelaide and Darwin (then called Palmerston). Searching for water, he discovered some springs which he named after his wife, Alice (now the location called Alice Springs).
   a. Charles Darwin
   b. Robert O'Hara Burke
   c. John MacDouall Stuart
   d. Charles Todd

10. This man donated his outstanding book collection to the NSW State Library. The part of the library housing the collection is named after him.
    a. David Scott Mitchell
    b. Joe Public
    c. Norman Lindsay
    d. Sir Thomas Lipton

FAMOUS AUSTRALIAN MEN

11. This man brought happiness to thousands of poor Aboriginal children at Christmas time as 'Black Santa'.
    a. Bennelong
    b. Charles Perkins
    c. Sydney Cunningham
    d. Ken Wyatt

12. The famous poet who wrote Waltzing Matilda was…..
    a. Henry Lawson
    b. Henry Kendall
    c. Adam Lindsay Gordon
    d. 'Banjo' Paterson

13. This man's bravery in Japanese prisoner of war camps during World War II inspired his fellow prisoners.
    a. Sir Thomas Blamey
    b. John Simpson Kirkpatrick
    c. Edward 'Weary' Dunlop
    d. Ned Kelly

14. This man's voice is known to most Australians. He has been a top-rating radio talkback host for over 40 years behind 'the Golden Microphone' (as he calls it).
    a. John Laws
    b. Mike Jeffreys
    c. Alan Jones
    d. Ron Casey

15. An outstanding sportsman and pastor of the Church of Christ, this man became our first Aboriginal Governor when appointed Governor of South Australia in 1976
    a. Albert Namatjira
    b. Sir Douglas (Pastor Doug) Nicholls
    c. Gary Foley
    d. Neville Bonner

16. With his wife, Elizabeth, this man wrote and illustrated numerous books about Australian birds. A league of bird lovers is named after him.
    a. Sir Joseph Banks
    b. John Gould
    c. Harry Butler
    d. Alfred Hitchcock

17. A great aviator who, in 1928, was the first to fly across the Pacific Ocean.
    a. Bert Hinkler
    b. Manfred von Richthofen
    c. Charles Kingsford Smith
    d. Algernon Bigglesworth

18. An Irishman who led the rebels against the payment for costly miners' licences in the Eureka Stockade at Ballarat in 1854.
    a. Edward Hargraves
    b. Harold Bell Lasseter
    c. Peter Lalor
    d. Paddy Hannan

19. With his partner, Joseph McGinnis, he turned a small, two-plane service into our national airline, QANTAS.
    a. Sir Hudson Fysh
    b. Sir Reginald Ansett
    c. Charles Ulm
    d. P G Taylor

20. This man spent many hours studying and crossbreeding wheat until he succeeded in growing varieties that resisted wheat diseases such as 'rust'.
    a. John MacArthur
    b. Sidney Kidman
    c. William Farrer
    d. James Ruse

....

24. THE HORROR FLIGHT OF BERTRAM & KLAUSMANN

During the early part of the twentieth century people were enthralled and amazed at the rapid developments in aviation. In a short space of time the idea of humans seeking to travel by means of flying had progressed from being an interesting novelty to an achievable reality. High stake flying races were held. Australians were prominent contributors to improvements in aviation.

In 1928 Bundaberg's Bert Hinkler had showed how durable and reliable aircraft could be by flying across the Pacific Ocean from England to Australia in just 15 days. Five years later Maude Rose (Lores) Bonney became to first woman to complete the flight from Australia to England. Charles Kingsford Smith was setting record after record flying over various routes and destinations.

The dizzying pace of change was probably far from prominent in the thoughts of Captain Hans Bertram on the morning of 14th May 1932. He was anxiously watching the fuel gauge on his sea plane as it emerged from clouds over the Timor Sea. He was hoping that he and his mechanic, Adolf Klausmann, could safely land somewhere on Australia's northern coastline. How great was the relief of both men when they caught sight of a sheltered inlet, landed in its shallows and taxied the aircraft to the shore.

With the landing safely negotiated both men shook hands with relief, confident that it would not be long before a search party would be sent to find them and rescue them. This confidence was to prove misguided.

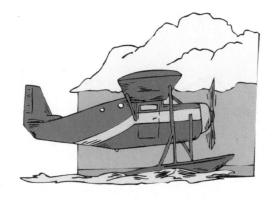

Bertram and Klausmann were from Germany. They had flown from the beautiful German cathedral city of Cologne in February of 1932. Their intention was to visit German communities along their route and promote Junkers aircraft parts and products in Australia. (Their sea plane was a Junkers Model W33.)

They were in Timor by May. Before them lay the most dangerous section of their flight. This was the crossing of the Timor Sea and landing in Darwin. Bad conditions dogged them from the start. Less than an hour into their journey a thick bank of clouds enveloped their Junkers. Unable to see to navigate and without the sophisticated equipment we have today, Bertram was forced to rely on his compass.

Dawn had not long broken when they cleared the cloud bank. In sight now, they thought, was the Australian North Coast. With the fuel gauge showing empty they put the plane down in the first inlet they saw. They believed they were on the north coast of Melville Island, a short distance to Darwin. Rescue, they reasoned, would not be far away.

That may have been the case had they been where they though they were. The truth, however, was that, lost in the cloud bank, they had wandered to a remote place 400 kilometres west of Darwin. This is one of the loneliest sections of coastline in the world. Thinking that Darwin was a moderate walk away they rested for a short time, filled a water bag used to cool the plane's engine and started their walk following the coastline eastwards.

A short distance into their journey the water bag failed. The precious drops could not be saved. They would have to find water along the way. Even so, they thought, a settlement or even Darwin itself, could not be far away. With the passing of every hour they began to understand that their initial calculations were wrong. No settlement or sign of human habitation made them realise that their calculations were a long way out. For the first time the thought that their lives may be played out in this remote and dreadful place was seen as a possibility.

On the third day of their trek eastwards, their throats parched with thirst, they found their way blocked by a tidal creek. Crossing it, they thought, would be tricky but manageable. They undressed and waded into the water, holding their garments and shoes overhead to prevent them from becoming wet.

Only when they were about half way across the creek did they notice three crocodiles on the opposite bank. At the same time the crocodiles noticed them. They slid down the muddy slope and were hurrying towards them. The clothing and footwear they had gone to such trouble to keep dry disappeared. The remainder of their progress would be naked — no shoes, no clothes.

Forced to turn back it took them four days to reach their abandoned plane. By now both men were suffering from terrible sunburn and had almost been bitten to death by stinging insects. Their only food had been a few small fish they were able to catch in shallow rock pools. These were eaten raw. Luckily a shower of rain had supplied them with some fresh drinking water.

Desparate to survive this ordeal, they converted one of the plane's floats into a boat. Perhaps they could paddle it close to a commonly used sea route and catch the attention of a passing boat. More in hope than in expectation, they paddled their craft out to sea. They continued for three days but, as their inner sense had told them, there were no boats to be seen. This was as remote a seaway as it was a highway.

Thirst, exhaustion and a rising swell that threatened to swamp their vessel convinced them to return to the shore. They had travelled a good distance west in their time at sea.

The remaining part of their 53 day ordeal is as terrible as the days that had preceded it. The ordeal ended when they were found by a rescue party from Wyndham. You can read the whole story in Hans Bertram's book, *Flight To Hell*. Klausmann returned to Germany by ship. He no longer felt safe flying. Bertram recovered the remnants of the sea plane and, after having it repaired and reassembled, flew it to Australia on a promotional tour.

While neither man looked back on their ordeal with fondness, they must, at times, marvel at the inner strength that allowed them to survive such an ordeal. Theirs is one of humankind's great survival stories.

COMPREHENSION

Write short answers below.

1. Write the dictionary definition of AVIATION. _____

   _____

2. From which Queensland city was Bert Hinkler? _____

3. From where to where was Hinkler's famous flight of 1928? _____

4. In which year did Maude Rose (Lores) Bonney fly from Australia to England?

   _____

5. Name another prominent aviator of the time? _____

6. Why were Hans Bertram and Adolf Klausmann anxious on the morning of 14th May 1932? _____

7. Where did they land their aeroplane? _____

8. From which country were they? _____

9. From which city had they flown? _____

10. What was the purpose of their flight? _____

11. What was the make and model of their aircraft? _____

12. What was the most dangerous section of their journey?_____

13. Why was it almost impossible to navigate the plane? _____

14. Where did they think they had landed? _____

15. How far, in fact, were they from Darwin? _____

16. What happened to the water bag when they had walked a short distance?

_____

17. What did they see when they were about half way across the tidal creek?

_____

18. What did they lose in the panic after seeing the crocodiles? _____

19. Name two things they were suffering from? _____

20. How long did it take them to return to their abandoned plane? _____

21. What did they eat? _____

22. What did they use for a boat? _____

23. What is the title of the book written by Hans Bertram? _____

24. Why did Klausmann return to Germany by boat? _____

_____

ANSWERS

1. SIR JOSEPH BANKS – COMPREHENSION

A.

1. Captain James Cook
2. Endeavour
3. 17 February 1743
4. science
5. Lincolnshire
6. botany
7. Harrow and Eton
8. Oxford University
9. The Royal Society
10. Labrador, Newfoundland
11. when the planet Venus passes directly between the sun and the Earth (and so blots the sun out for a time
12. Australia's East Coast
13. they were unable to raise the necessary funds
14. Iceland and the Hebrides Islands
15. New South Wales
16. a settlement party of soldiers and convicts went to NSW
17. Arthur Phillip
18. gout
19. Banksia, Banksmeadow, Bankstown
20. the Father of Australia

B.

a. Banksmeadow = 3
b. Newfoundland = 8
c. Australia = 1
d. Banksia = 2
e. Labrador = 7
f. Bankstown = 4
g. Hebrides Islands
h. Iceland = 6

C.

1. fortune
2. science
3. provide
4. further
5. lobbying

SIR JOSEPH BANKS – ENRICHMENT

A.

1. avocado
2. deciduous
3. flora
4. botany
5. suburb
6. biology
7. grassland
8. chlorophyll
9. palm
10. cosmopolitan
11. foetid
12. leaves

PUZZLE : Very big hands.

B.

1. exotic
2. Venus
3. lacking
4. prefix
5. epidermis
6. forest

PUZZLE : tulips (two lips)

2. MAJOR JAMES MUDIE – COMPREHENSION

A.

1. he was a disastrous leader and was ordered to resign
2. a bookseller
3. medallions
4. great English leaders / battles with the armies of of the French emperor, Napoleon
5. £10 000 ($20 000)
6. Sir Charles Forbes
7. 870 hectares
8. Patrick's Plains on the Hunter River
9. Castle Forbes
10. convict
11. he hanged five convicts who were working for him
12. Maitland
13. because it acted as a deterrent to the lower classes in England
14. (c) poor people
15. grass seeds and sweepings from the floor of the mill
16. the tough, leathery meat of an old bullock
17. they were caught, five were hanged and the other sentenced to life imprisonment on Norfolk Island
18. Sydney Gazette
19. William Watt (a former convict)
20. living with a convict woman
21. The Felonry Of New South Wales
22. John Kinchela
23. they paid the £50 fine imposed by the court
24. England, 1852

B.

1. detested
2. disliked
3. labourers
4. smirked
5. magistrate

MAJOR JAMES MUDIE
ENRICHMENT CRIME & PUNISHMENT

1. fine
2. jaywalking
3. arson
4. vandal
5. collar
6. bribery
7. fraud
8. community
9. blasphemy
10. trespass
11. offence
12. libel
13. prevaricate
14. assault
15. hijacking
16. polygamy

PUZZLE: FYODOR DOSTOEVSKY is the author of Crime & Punishment

Embezzlement = theft of money placed in one's trust or belonging to one's employer

3. PLAGUE IN SYDNEY!

COMPREHENSION

1. 1349, 1666
2. 1900
3. Paul-Louis Simond
4. Hong Kong, Malaysia, Japan, Philippines and India
5. Noumea
6. Dr John Thompson
7. they were riddled (badly infected) with plague
8. an extermination campaign
9. Arthur
10. a carter on the wharves at Darling Harbour
11. a sailmaker who worked on the wharves
12. under the floorboards
13. 100 000
14. headache, fever, vomiting
15. delirium
16. lymph nodes become swollen, pustulent black sores break out on the skin
17. a few hours
18. wash woodwork with lime and carbolic acid
19. Brisbane, Rockhampton, Townsville, Melbourne, Fremantle
20. 9th August, 1900
21. 303
22. 103
23. 1902, 1921
24. plague = an infectious disease spread to humans by rat fleas; any widespread outbreak of a highly infectious disease

PLAGUE IN SYDNEY! ENRICHMENT ACTIVITY

1. zoonosis
2. infectious
3. vector
4. epidemic
5. pandemic
6. mosquito
7. mortality
8. fracture
9. antibiotic
10. pathogen
11. incubation
12. outbreak
13. ophthalmologist
14. surgeon
15. malignant
16. chronic
17. thrombosis
18. sprain
19. diagnosis
20. midwife

RIDDLE: Sure ! Come back tomorrow!

4. CHRISTMAS IN EARLY SYDNEY

COMPREHENSION

A.

1. a Christmas song
2. jolly
3. Summer
4. mouldy biscuits, salted meat, swigs of rum
5. chaplain Richard Johnson
6. under a gum tree near the Tank Stream
7. a convict was sentenced to 200 lashes
8. he was hanged
9. he died of self-imposed starvation
10. marriages
11. Lord Howe Island turtles
12. James Daley
13. he was hanged
14. her hair was shaved off and she was paraded before the assembled convicts in a canvas frock with the letters R S G painted on it
15. receiver of stolen goods
16. twelve kilograms
17. completely insane
18. 1790
19. more than 250
20. 500
21. South Africa
22. 30 tonnes of rice, ½ a tonne of sugar, 50 barrels of salted beef or pork
23. 44° C
24. the blast of a heated oven
25. 11th December 1792

B. Teacher

CHRISTMAS IN EARLY SYDNEY – ENRICHMENT

A.

1. Manger
2. Joy
3. Donkey
4. Gentlemen
5. Drum
6. Tree
7. City
8. Mary
9. Silent
10. Orient

B. Teacher

C.

1. Charles Dickens
2. London
3. Ebenezer
4. Tiny Tim

D. Great Expectations, Oliver Twist, Bleak House, David Copperfield, Pickwick Papers

E. Teacher

5. THE MYSTERY DISAPPEARANCE OF THE 'KICKING KANGAROO'

COMPREHENSION

A.

1. Mordialloc Beach
2. a shark was approaching about 30 metres away
3. 15 years old
4. Royal Humane Society Of Australasia
5. American football, gridiron
6. 18th March 1872 in the Victorian town of Kilmore
7. Xavier College in Melbourne
8. Melbourne, Essondon
9. Oxford University
10. law
11. University of Wisconsin
12. the field is marked out like a gridiron used for grilling meat
13. kicking
14. quarterback
15. The Kicking Kangaroo
16. coach
17. Notre Dame University and Stanford University
18. he disappeared mysteriosly
19. joined the Australian army as it passed through San Francisco on its way to the World War I battle front
20. 17 years
21. San Francisco Chronicle
22. Charles J Mitchell
23. a lumber company in the isolated town of Westwood, California
24. they welcomed his return
25. 1962
26. John F Kennedy

B. 160 points

THE MYSTERY DISAPPEARANCE OF THE 'KICKING KANGAROO' AUSTRALIAN SPORTING HEROES

1. (b) Greg Norman
2. (c) Pat O'Day
3. (a) netball
4. (b) Don Bradman
5. (d) Des Renford
6. (c) Fanny Durack
7. (c) Cliff Young
8. (b) Grand Flaneur
9. (d) Tony Lockett
10. (b) Frank Beaurepaire
11. (a) McGilvray
12. (d) John Bertrand
13. (a) Brian Bevan
14. (c) Sir Jack Brabham
15. (a) Jim Pike
16. (d) Walter Lindrum
17. Henry 'Bobby'Pearce
18. (b) Heather McKay
19. (b) Decima Norman
20. (c) Hubert Opperman
21. (b) Ella Brothers
22. (d) Beetson
23. (a) Cadell Evans
24. (d) Craig Johnston
25. (a) Mark Richards

6. MATTHEW FLINDERS AND CAPTAIN PALMER COMPREHENSION

A.

1. map Australia's east coast
2. 1803
3. Australia was a large island
4. two smaller islands
5. they were regarded as being honourable men who cared about the welfare of their sailor
6. HMS Porpoise
7. HMS Cato, HMS Bridgewater
8. a reef
9. Bridgewater
10. it sailed away from them
11. on a spit close to the reef
12. 100m long and 50m wide
13. when the tide fell
14. three
15. 500 kilometres from what is now Rockhampton
16. he could not be relied on
17. Hope
18. thirteen days
19. he wrote that they had both sunk with no survivors
20. it vanished and was never seen again

B. **POSITIVE:** compassionate, helpful, courageous

NEGATIVE: traitorous, apathetic, cowardly

MATTHEW FLINDERS AND CAPTAIN PALMER ENRICHMENT

1. tramp steamer
2. hawser
3. rudder
4. starboard
5. hull
6. mariner
7. poop
8. bow
9. wake
10. stern
11. aft
12. sampan
13. junk
14. bridge
15. amidships
16. kayak
17. rowlock
18. brig
19. conning tower
20. dreadnought
21. log
22. berth
23. Blue Peter
24. skipper
25. capstan

PUZZLE 1: The ship was a submarine.

PUZZLE 2: It was full of leeks.

7. THE AMAZING JOURNEY OF OSKAR SPECK COMPREHENSION

A.
1. electrical contractor
2. twenty-one
3. World War I and the Great Depression
4. close his factory
5. a fold-up kayak
6. more than seven years
7. Sunnschien
8. Cyprus
9. Mediterranean
10. Germany, India, Sri Lanka, Burma, Thailand, Malaysia, Indonesia, New Guinea, Australia
11. Australia
12. tied him up, kicked and beat him, stole most of his supplies
13. the world was at war
14. a spy
15. placed him in an internment camp
16. Lightning Ridge in New South Wales
17. opal cutting
18. opal merchant
19. 1945
20. Australian National Maritime Museum at Darling Harbour in Sydney

B.
1. enterprising
2. destination
3. initial
4. makeshift
5. furthermore
6. internment

THE AMAZING JOURNEY OF OSKAR SPECK ENRICHMENT ACTIVITY

1. Square Mile
2. Teardrop
3. Emerald
4. Eternal
5. O'Groats
6. Cloud
7. Apple
8. Motown
9. Canals
10. Tinsel Town
11. Lusitania
12. Big
13. Holy
14. Huns
15. Windy
16. Hibernia
17. Subcontinent
18. Skeleton
19. Rising Sun

PUZZLE: stars dancing on water

8. THE HOLDEN STORY – COMPREHENSION

1. England, Staffordshire
2. leatherworking
3. James Alexander Holden
4. making and repairing leather harness / repairing carriages
5. he was restless / ambitious / he did not get on with his stepmother
6. Adelaide
7. twenty
8. hardware shop
9. he had a reputation for being skilful craftsman
10. Hindley Street
11. making coach bodies and fittings
12. Grenfell Street
13. more than forty years
14. a large wooden horse
15. Henry Adolf Frost
16. Germany
17. 1887
18. 1859
19. Boer War
20. farmer
21. South Africa
22. 10 000 sets of saddles and harness for mounted soldiers
23. Norwood
24. things were set up seemingly overnight
25. mayor of Norwood

26. horseless carriages
27. the car (automobile)
28. Ford and Dodge
29. Woodville
30. 1948

8. THE HOLDEN STORY
ENRICHMENT ACTIVITY

1. convertible
2. fender
3. Steamer
4. speedometer
5. brakes
6. trunk
7. jack
8. seatbelt
9. licence
10. global
11. automatic
12. bio
13. manual
14. reverse
15. traffic
16. carriage
17. accelerator
18. horn
19. rear
20. bonnet
21. headlights
22. dipstick
23. blinkers
24. panel

PUZZLE: INTERNAL COMBUSTION ENGINE

9. GEORGE PENCHEFF – PIONEER WRESTLER

COMPREHENSION

A.
1. Russia
2. wrestling
3. they were thrown out of the ring by the winner
4. a Turkish Shepherd
5. thirteen
6. less than thirty seconds
7. a baby bull
8. more than five thousand
9. twenty-eight
10. 1927
11. lifted a car and 25 men together
12. Mildura
13. three days
14. Roy McKinnon (the local idol)
15. Lew Laconeo
16. a broken arm
17. King Kong from Singapore, Don Koloff, Johannes Vanderwalt, Jim Londos
18. two hours
19. held his arm in the air
20. wrestled in front of a crowd of 140 000 fans in India

21. the Russian Rocket
22. they rushed him and kissed his feet
23. in the early 1960s
24. ten thousand

B. his father was a very big man

C.
1. modest
2. victor
3. powerful
4. bout

GEORGE PENCHEFF – PIONEER WRESTLER ACTIVITY

10. THE PRIME MINISTER WHO LOVED THE SEA

COMPREHENSION

1. Sunday 17th December 1967
2. Alec Rose
3. Melbourne
4. A yawl is a two masted sailing vessel rigged fore and aft with a large mainmast and a small mizzenmast.

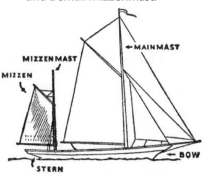

Mizzen and mizzenmast on a yawl

5. Lively Lady
6. Cheviot Beach
7. the passenger steamer, Cheviot
8. snorkelling
9. swimming trunks, sandshoes
10. Yes, because he said, 'I know this beach like the back of my hand. '
11. the roaring waters drowned out her calls
12. like a leaf being taken out
13. the Army Officer Cadet School at Portsea
14. 1.56pm
15. eight
16. three hundred
17. 696 days
18. Sir John McKewen
19. Lyndon Baines Johnson
20. ' …that there will be a corner of your mind and heart which takes cheer from the fact that you have an admiring friend, a staunch friend, that will be all the way with L B J.'
21. LBJ are the initials for Lyndon Baines Johnson
22. he was a Chinese spy and a submarine had taken him back to China

23. the strong current pulled his body far out to sea / he was eaten by sharks
24. the sea

THE PRIME MINISTER WHO LOVED THE SEA ACTIVITY

A.
1. overcast
2. experienced
3. concerned
4. popular
5. funeral
6. cheer

B.
a. 4
b. 1
c. 5
d. 3
e. 2
f. 6

C. a belief that a bad happening is the result of a secret plan carried out by powerful people
D. teacher
E. Edmund Barton, Alfred Deakin, Chris Watson, Sir George Reid, Andrew Fisher

11. PERCY GRAINGER – COMPREHENSION

A.
1. laughter and enjoyment
2. joyful noise
3. England
4. Rose Aldridge
5. 1882
6. alcohol
7. a music teacher
8. Percy (her son)
9. twelve years
10. three months
11. Viking myths and legends
12. violent and flamboyant
13. red
14. Professor Louis Pabet
15. Frankfurt
16. music school
17. she fell and injured herself when ice skating
18. London
19. his mother
20. * he would cease playing and tell the audience some anecdotes about his life * he would push his piano to a part of the stage where he thought the sound quality might be better
21. he would often run from his home to a concert (recital)
22. it saved him money and he enjoyed the exercise
23. painful sores on the fingertips
24. helping the ship's stoker shovel coal for the engine
25. Ada Crossly

26. walking from venue to venue
27. he would arrive at a concert only a few minutes before it was due to start
28. Edvard Grieg
29. The Peer Gynt Suite
30. Danny Boy, In An English Country Garden
31. his mother ended her life by jumping from the eighteenth storey window of a New York building
32. he could store dirty linen inside it

PERCY GRAINGER ACTIVITY

A. 88 keys, 52 white, 36 black
B.
1. hard, white substance that is found in the tusks of elephants, walrus etc
2. playing the piano

C.
1. pianist
2. violinist
3. flautist
4. cellist
5. saxophonist
6. harpist
7. tubist
8. trumpeter
9. banjo player
10. guitarist

D.
1. mandolin
2. xylophone
3. cymbal
4. viola
5. harmonica
6. drum
7. clarinet
8. banjo
9. bagpipes
10. bassoon
11. harp
12. recorder
13. castanet (more commonly used in the plural, castanets
14. piccolo
15. trumpet
16. cornet
17. violin
18. piano
19. tuba
20. organ

What happened? : Nero was a Roman Emperor. Some versions of history depict him as being very vain and arrogant. He is said to have thought himself a great artist and musician. During The Great Fire Of Rome, in 64 AD, he is said to have been so captured by his own playing of the violin (also called *a fiddle*) that he hardly noticed the fire. This is a play on words. A *fiddle* is another name for a violin. To **fiddle** can also mean to waste one's time in idle play.

12. SYDNEY CUNNINGHAM OAM THE BLACK SANTA

COMPREHENSION

A.
1. the Yuen Aboriginal people
2. South Coast of New South Wales
3. Aboriginal children from poor families around NSW
4. red overalls, a red pyjama top and gumboots
5. over 6 000
6. ring radio and television stations
7. a chair, table and bucket
8. a helicopter
9. Papua New Guinea
10. ANZAC Of The Year
11. Australian Aboriginal Of The Year
12. Order Of Australia Medal (OAM)

B.

C.
1. gentlemen
2. high
3. night
4. Noel
5. faithful
6. world
7. manger

D. Teacher

SYDNEY CUNNINGHAM OAM ABORIGINAL ACHIEVERS
1. 'Mum Shirl '
2. Neville Bonner
3. Archie Roach
4. Sir (Pastor) Douglas Nicholls
5. Eddie Mabo
6. Galmahra (Jackey Jackey)
7. Albert Namatjira
8. Harold Blair
9. Kyle Vander-Kuyp
10. Lionel Rose
11. David Unaipon
12. Graham 'Polly 'Farmer
13. Ernie Dingo
14. Oodgeroo Noonuccal
15. Charles Perkins
16. Evonne Cawley (Goolagong)
17. Cathy Freeman
18. Mal Meninga
19. David Gulpilil
20. the Ella Brothers

13. THE ANIMALS' FRIEND – COMPREHENSION

A.
1. calves that had become lost or been abandoned by their mothers
2. Charles Lort Smith
3. how animals were treated
4. four thousand
5. an ambulance
6. the displays were rebuilt so that the animals were more humanely housed
7. they were unable to speak up for themselves
8. over five million

B. The good person is the friend of all animals.

C. generous caring determined kind persistent

D.
1. prominent
2. proposed
3. humanely
4. enacted
5. graphically

E. teacher

THE ANIMALS' FRIEND ANIMALS IN STRANGE PLACES
1. tiger
2. hawk
3. monkey
4. wolf
5. eagle
6. rabbit
7. goat(ee)
8. crocodile
9. hare
10. dove

Riddle 1: the letter 'e '
11. cat
12. kiwi
13. crab
14. turtle
15. zebra
16. horse
17. worm
18. spider
19. lion
20. fox
21. pony

Riddle 2: a watermelon
22. beetle
23. loan
24. kangaroo
25. snake
26. duck

27. bee
28. donkey
29. spider
30. sheep
31. canary

Riddle 3: bookkeeper

14. LES DARCY – COMPREHENSION

A.
1. Don Bradman, Phar Lap, Les Darcy
2. near Maitland, NSW
3. blacksmith's striker
4. Mick Hawkins, Tim Sullivan
5. middleweight
6. Al McCoy
7. compulsory service for one's country (usually military service)
8. because he did not enlist in the army
9. he was under twenty-one and his parents did not give him consent to enlist
10. War Precautions Act
11. two infected teeth
12. Winnie O'Sullivan

B.
1. mighty
2. handsome
3. tremendous
4. enormous

C. shirker Chile pneumonia national

D.
1. approaching
2. stowaway
3. shirker
4. able bodied

14. LES DARCY – BOXING ACTIVITY

A. Heavyweight = unlimited, Cruiserweight = 90.7kg , Light Heavyweight = 79.4kg , Middleweight = 72.5kg, Welterweight = 66.7kg , Lightweight = 61.2kg, Featherweight = 57.2kg, Bantamweight = 53.5kg, Flyweight = 50.8kg
B. the rules that govern boxing contests
C. brain disorder caused by repeated blows to the head, typically in boxing matches; symptoms include slurred speech, a lack of co-ordination and general confusion
D. teacher

15. DOCTOR GEORGE BORNEMISSZA ACTIVITY / RESEARCH SHEET

1. Commonwealth Scientific And Industrial Research Organisation
a. six
b. teacher
c. Budapest
d. house fly, horse fly, March fly, blowfly are a few
e. a popular singing group of the 1960s comprising John Lennon, Paul McCartney, George Harrison and Ringo Starr

2.
a. archaeology
b. zoology
c. anatomy
d. biology
e. geology
f. meteorology
g. astronomy
h. botany
i. geography
j. entomology
k. ornithology
l. geometry
m. bacteriology
n. pharmacology

BIOLOGICAL CONTROL COMPREHENSION

1.
a. cane toad
b. it had no natural enemies
c. 24 wild English rabbits
d. myxomatosis
e. spreading quickly within a population (of a disease)
f. cactus
g. cactoblastis
h. sheep
i. dung beetles
j. assassin bug

** Note: Australia has its own native dung beetles but cow and sheep droppings were not tempting to them.

2.
a. using natural predators rather than poison sprays to control plant and animal pest numbers
b. to control sugar cane beetles
c. blowflies lay eggs directly onto sheep (usually around the anus which is not readily accessible to the sheep) – when the eggs hatch the maggots will often burrow into the living sheep eventually causing infection – these sheep usually die as a result
d. buries dung balls reducing sites where blowflies can lay their eggs

3.
a. devise
b. leaches
c. orchard
d. ruined
e. assassin
f. dung
g. maggots
h. reduces
i. released PATERSON'S CURSE: a plant pest which when eaten by sheep or cattle kills them or makes them very sick – beekeepers call it SALVATION JANE as it is a very good honey yielding plant

16. JAMES JOHNSON AND FREDERICK HEDGES — SURVIVORS COMPREHENSION

A.
1. Sydney Heads (North Head and South Head)
2. 1857
3. James Johnson
4. 121
5. twenty-four
6. the entrance to Newcastle Harbour
7. the Oyster Banks
8. he held onto a buoy
9. fifty-nine
10. one sole-survivor helped rescue another

B. 1. site 2. visibility 3. error 4. debris 5. co-incidence

C. 1 = 2 2 = 7 3 = 4 4 = 2 5 = 6 6 = 3 7 = 5

17. ALBERT NAMATJIRA

ACTIVITY / COMPREHENSION

A.
1. fact
2. opinion
3. opinion
4. fact
5. opinion

B.
1. Cattle raising became unprofitable … Aborigines began making souvenirs to sell.
2. Rex Battarbee visited Hermannsburg… Albert got some training in the use of watercolours.
3. Elders and missionaries disapproved of his marriage…Albert and Ilkalita ran away.
4. Albert's paintings made him some money…the Taxation Department pursued Albert.
5. A law did not allow aborigines into Adelaide after dark…Albert was unable to build a house in Adelaide.

C. teacher

D.
1. Lutheran
2. tribal
3. souvenirs
4. Battarbee
5. exhibitions
6. discriminatory

E. *grew up on mission run by church * learnt Christian and tribal teachings *first signs artistic talent showed when mission making souvenirs showed *artist Rex Battarbee gave Albert lessons watercolours *Albert began make money after exhibitions *unable do things discriminatory laws

18. PHAR LAP

COMPREHENSION

A.
1. closed down
2. people lost their jobs
3. cycling
4. cricket
5. billiards and snooker
6. lightning (in Thai)
7. Thailand
8. Harry Telford
9. David J Davis
10. Bobby
11. Tommy Woodcock
12. Jim Pike
13. first Tuesday in November
14. 1930
15. dew covered alfalfa caused gas to build up in his stomach
16. Museum Victoria

B. CLIMAX = the most intense, exciting or important point; the pinnacle
ANTICLIMAX = a disappointing end to an exciting series of events

C.
1. sire = male parent, dam = female parent
2. Night Raid
3. Entreaty

19. DON BRADMAN
COMPREHENSION CROSSWORD

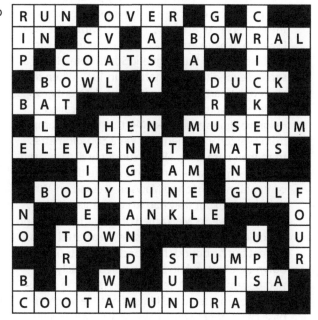

20. JOHN SIMPSON (KIRKPATRICK) COMPREHENSION CROSSWORD

ACTIVITY PROPAGANDA

1. The first aims to shame the father into enlisting so that his son will not see him as a shirker and coward.
2. This poster dehumanises the German as being no more than a made brute, not a person with any measure of civilisation, culture or feelings.
3. to characterise a person or group in an over simplified (usually wrong) way
4. to remove a person's human qualities; to depict them as having no human qualities apart from a distorted physical likeness

21. SIR DOUGLAS MAWSON COMPREHENSION / CLOSE

Mawson came to Australia with his parents when he was a child. He became a lecturer in mineralogy at the University of Adelaide. He went with Edgeworth David to explore Antarctica. This expedition was the first to reach the Magnetic South Pole. He led a second expedition to Antarctica in 1911. When they arrived the party broke up into five different groups. In Mawson's group was and Englishman called Belgrave Ninnis and Xavier Mertz, a skiing champion from Switzerland.When they were 500 kilometres from their base camp Ninnis suddenly disappeared into a deep crevasse. Unable to rescue their companion, Merttz and Mawson pressed on. When their food ran out they had to eat the sled dogs. After three weeks Mertz died of starvation. Mawson struggled on by himself. His soles separated from his feet but he bound them back on. He, too, fell down a crevasse while pulling a sled. Luckily the sled became stuck. After dangling from the straps for some time he pulled himself out. He reached base camp after twenty days, only to see his ship, the Aurora vanishing over the horizon. Luckily some men had stayed behind in the hope that he would return.

22. FRED HOLLOWS COMPREHENSION

A.

1. enthusiasm to do something
2. looking after the old, the lame and the blind
3. 1929, New Zealand
4. 1965
5. Medicine
6. Northern Territory
7. aboriginal stockmen
8. Labrador keratopathy
9. lack of protection from the sun as they worked outside all day
10. blindness
11. National Trachoma And Eye Health Program
12. 30 000
13. Order Of Australia
14. it would send the signal that aboriginal health was being adequately attended to
15. Vietnam, Burma (Myanmar), Thailand, Eritrea
16. Eritrea
17. cancer
18. 1993
19. Bourke
20. the outback

B.

1. dentist
2. oculist
3. audiologist
4. gastrologist
5. nephrologist
6. osteologist
7. neurologist
8. cardiologist
9. haematologist
10. dermatologist

FRED HOLLOWS ENRICHMENT ACTIVITY

A.

1. teacher
2. among people of no talent someone with a little talent is seen as being special

B. teacher

23. AUSTRALIAN SONGBIRDS ACTIVITY

A.

1. Helen Porter Mitchell
2. after her home city, Melbourne
3. Europe
4. Peach Melba, Melba Toast
5. to announce one's retirement but then make many comebacks
6. that they were as good as any in the world
7. Townsville
8. Our Glad

9. June Gough
10. Broken Hill
11. La Stupenda
12. the Wonderful One

B.
1. On The Road To Gundagai
2. Our Don Bradman
3. Advance Australia Fair
4. Waltzing Matilda
5. The Drover's Dream
6. I've Been Everywhere

C. STATEMENT: June Gough was born in Broken Hill.
QUESTION: Was June Gough born in Broken Hill?

D. population, farewell, pioneer, example, serving, gratitude, enriches

FAMOUS AUSTRALIAN WOMEN

1. (a) Mary Reiby
2. (c) Kay Cottee
3. (a) Maude Rose (Lores) Bonney
4. (c) Nancy Wake
5. (b) Dorothea MacKellar
6. (d) Vivian Bullwinkle
7. (a) Colleen McCullough
8. Patricia O'Shane
9. (b) Dame Enid Lyons
10. Annette Kellerman
11. (c) Grace Bussell
12. (d) Elle MacPherson
13. (a) Louise Sauvage
14. (c) May Gibbs
15. (a) Cathy Freeman
16. (a) Maree Lyndon
17. (b) Edith Cowan
18. (a) Julia Gillard
19. (a) Mavis Bramston
20. (c) Dame Peggy Van Praagh

FAMOUS AUSTRALIAN MEN

1. (b) Edmund Barton
2. (b) Blaxland, Lawson And Wentworth
3. (a) Burke And Wills
4. (d) John Curtin
5. (b) Sir Roden Cutler
6. (c) Steele Rudd
7. (a) Joern Utzon
8. (a) Sir MacFarlane Burnet
9. (d) Charles Todd
10. (a) David Scott Mitchell
11. (c) Sydney Cunningham
12. (d) 'Banjo ' Paterson
13. (c) Edward 'Weary ' Dunlop
14. (a) John Laws
15. (b) Sir Douglas (Pastor Doug) Nicholls
16. (b) John Gould
17. (a) Bert Hinkler
18. (c) Peter Lalor
19. (a) Sir Hudson Fysh
20. (c) William Farrer

24. THE HORROR FLIGHT OF BERTRAM & KLAUSMANN

1. the science of flying aircraft
2. Bundaberg
3. from England to Australia
4. 1933 (inferential question)
5. Charles Kingsford Smith is mentioned in the article; students may choose others a
6. their aeroplane was running very low on fuel
7. in a small inlet on Australia's northern coastline
8. Germany
9. Cologne
10. to visit German communities and promote Junkers aeroplane products
11. W33
12. crossing the Timor Sea and landing in Darwin
13. lack of visibility due to a widespread cloud bank
14. on the North coast of Melville Island (a short distance from Darwin)
15. 400 kilometres
16. it burst (failed)
17. three crocodiles
18. their shoes and clothing
19. sunburn, insect stings
20. four days
21. small fish caught in shallow rock pools
22. a float from the plane
23. Flight To Hell
24. he no longer felt safe flying